John McArthur

The Antiquities of Arran

John McArthur

The Antiquities of Arran

ISBN/EAN: 9783744716963

Printed in Europe, USA, Canada, Australia, Japan

Cover: Foto ©ninafisch / pixelio.de

More available books at **www.hansebooks.com**

THE

ANTIQUITIES OF ARRAN.

Fingal's and Bruce's Cave.

THE

ANTIQUITIES OF ARRAN:

WITH A

Historical Sketch of the Island,

EMBRACING AN ACCOUNT OF

THE SUDREYJAR UNDER THE NORSEMEN.

BY

JOHN M'ARTHUR.

"Enquire, I pray thee, of the former age, and prepare thyself to the search of their fathers: for we are but of yesterday."—Job viii. 8, 9.

Illustrated by James Napier, Jun.

GLASGOW: THOMAS MURRAY AND SON.
EDINBURGH: PATON AND RITCHIE.
LONDON: ARTHUR HALL, VIRTUE AND CO.
1861.

PREFATORY NOTE.

WHILST spending a few days in Arran, the attention of the Author was drawn to the numerous pre-historic monuments scattered over the Island.

The present small Work embraces an account of these interesting remains, prepared chiefly from careful personal observation.

The concluding Part contains a description of the monuments of a later period—the chapels and castles of the Island—to which a few brief historical notices have been appended.

Should the persual of these pages induce a more thorough investigation into these stone-records of the ancient history of Arran, the object of the Author shall have been amply attained.

The Author begs here gratefully to acknowledge the kindness and assistance rendered him by JOHN BUCHANAN, Esq. of Glasgow; JAMES NAPIER, Esq., F.C.S., &c., Killin; the Rev. COLIN F. CAMPBELL of Kilbride, and the Rev. CHARLES STEWART, Kilmorie—Arran.

4 RADNOR TERRACE,
GLASGOW, *June*, 1861.

CONTENTS.

ILLUSTRATIONS.

B

PART I.

STONE PERIOD.

CHAPTER I.

Introduction.

The Island of Arran* lies at the mouth of the Frith of Clyde, and forms one of the *Sudreyjar*, or Southern Hebrides.

It is twenty-four miles in length, by ten to twelve in breadth, and is divided by a *string* of heath-clad hills into the parishes of Kilbride on the east and Kilmorie on the west. Its shores are rocky and precipitous, here and there fringed to the water's edge with feathery brushwood, and indented by the Bays of Brodick, Lamlash, Whiting, Mauchrie, and Ranza.

From the summit of Ben Gnuis, or better still, from the granite brow of Ben Ghaioul, the *coup d'œil* is magnificent in the extreme. To the north, rugged cliffs, mountain corries,

---

* Glotta—Hersey—Arram—Aran—Arane—Arrane—Aren—Arran —*Ar*, a land; *rin*, sharp points.

and dark ravines, open beneath us.   The peaks of Cior Mhor,
Casdael Abhael, and Suidhe Fheargus, rise bare and grim.
A light fleecy mist veils the paps of the Ciodh-na-oigh—
Maiden's Breast.   Beyond is the sweep of the eastern shore,
with the waves surging on the golden sands of the Bay of
Sannox.   The islands of Bute and the Cumbraes sleep peacefully on the glistening waters; and stretching still northwards are the straggling lochs and lakes of Argyll and the
surf-beaten Hebrides.   To the east is seen the clear outline of
the Ayrshire coast, with its sandy bays, busy harbours, and old
castles; and in the extreme distance, the white smoke resting
over the towns and hamlets of the shires of Lanark and
Renfrew.   Southwards are the purple ridges of the Ross and
the Faerie hills; the Holy Isle guarding the Bay of Lamlash;
the gray ruins of Kildonan Peel; the Craig of Ailsa looming
like a spectre on the blue waves; and the dim shadowy outline of the Irish coast beyond.

Over the *string* of swelling heights, which intersect the
island from north to south, the wild Highland features of the
eastern coast are changed for the more regular characteristics
of lowland scenery.   Heath-clad hills stretch in gentle undu-
lation along the coast, whilst fields of emerald pasture and
waving grain, and wastes of moorland, extend along the
shore levels; with here and there a few village cots clustering around the bays and within the glens.

But Arran must be examined and studied in detail to
elicit all the richness and variety of its attractions.   It offers
an inexhaustible treasury of material for the zoologist, the
geologist, and the botanist, amongst the crannies of the rocks

at low water, along the shelving cliffs of the coast, and amidst the heathery nooks and woody dingles of the glens and hills and mountain streamlets.

The rocks and the woodlands have their own peculiar charm;—the botanist may wander over the fields, the moors, and the flowery dells, and gather, year by year, fresh laurels with which to adorn the storehouse of his science; the geologist may re-clothe the primeval world, with its virgin forests; trace out in the old strata the footprints of extinct mammalia, and from a few fossil remains reconstruct their huge proportions. But there is a later and a higher formation which "pieces on in natural sequence to the geology," which has for us a deeper and more kindred interest. Buried amidst the heath, and hoary with the moss of ages, we discover the rude monumental remains of primeval man—the sole records which time has left us of his early history.

The old gray cairns, the lichen-covered monoliths, the ruined forts and cells and castles of early times, lie scattered about in almost every dingle, glen, and moor of Arran. Many a wild and weird tradition hovers over these old monuments; but the origin and history of the cairn and monolith builders remain shrouded in the mists of the past. That they were an earlier people than the Celtæ is now generally admitted by ethnologists; and to distinguish them from the Indo-European tribes, whom they preceded, Dr Prichard has applied to them the somewhat hypothetical designation of "Allophylian." *

* Dr Prichard's Natural History of Man, page 186; Wilson's Archæology, page 161.

It would be mere idle conjecture to attempt to indicate, with any degree of certainty, the time when these rude colonists—emerging from their cradle-land in the East, and wandering over the vast forest-lands of the European Continent—landed in their fire-hollowed canoes upon the shores of the British Isles. It is more than probable, however, that long before King Chufu had commenced to build the great pyramid on the banks of the Nile, the rude Allophylian was rearing the barrow, the cromlech, and the stone circle, around the coasts of the Hebrides and within the glens of the Scottish mainland.

But remote as these monuments are in their antiquity, the world has been now and again startled by the traces of the works of man, existing at a period apparently long prior to the first dawn of Adamic history. In 1797 several flint weapons were found in Suffolk, mingled with the bones of extinct mammalia, at a depth of eleven to twelve feet below the surface soil. Similar discoveries have been made in the gravel beds of Peterborough; on the coast of Ayrshire; in the Brixham Cave, Devonshire; in the caves of Sicily, and other places. About four years ago a series of borings were made in the deposits of the river Nile. "In the lowest part of the sediment, at the colossal statue of Memphis, at the depth of thirty-nine feet from the surface of the ground, consisting of true Nilotic sediment, the instrument brought up a fragment of pottery. Having been found at the depth of thirty-nine feet, it would seem to be a true record of the existence of man 13,371 years before A.D. 1854—reckoning by the before-mentioned rate of increase, seventy-three and a half inches in a century."*

Whilst we attach but little importance to the finding of an isolated fragment of pottery in the Nilotic deposits, the discoveries of M. Boucher de Perthes, of flint instruments, in the neighbourhood of Abbeville and Amiens, recently investigated and verified by Mr Prestwich and other eminent geologists, are deserving of more serious attention. These implements consist of flakes of flint, broken and chipped into the forms of knives, arrow-heads, spear or lance-heads, and axes, all unquestionably of human workmanship.

They have been disinterred from undisturbed beds of Drift, at an elevation of about two hundred feet above the sea level, superimposed by a layer of grayish sand—containing the shells of fresh-water mallusca—and a bed of brown brick earth, or ferruginous clay, or loam. Large quantities of these rude instruments have been found, discoloured and incrusted by their contact with ochreous matter and carbonate of lime. The bones of extinct mammalia, including the elephant, the rhinoceros, the bear, the hyena, and the tiger, have been discovered on the adjacent hills; and the entire evidence is suggestive of the existence of a rude and barbarous people, coeval with the huge mammalia, which prowled amidst the forests and jungles of the old world, probably before the British Islands were disunited from the continent of Europe.†

* Communication by L. Horner, Esq., V.P.R.S., to the Royal Society, 11th February, 1858.

† "I am warranted in asserting, that the most sceptical visitor to M. de Perthes' museum, will go away a convert to the opinion that the

The implement remains of the sons of the Drift are distinctive and peculiar in their formation, and possess but little resemblance to the beautifully polished arrow-heads and hatchets of stone and flint of the Allophylian and Celtic races.

We may reasonably conclude, therefore, that the rude Allophyliæ, who at a remote period inhabited our island, were preceded by an older and still more barbarous people, respecting whose origin and history we are entirely ignorant.

When the adventurous Allophyliæ first landed upon the shores of Arran, vast forests, infested by beasts of prey, covered the face of the island; dusky tarns glimmered in the deep corries of its glens, and along its coasts the ocean waves were still gnawing its sandstone cliffs into abodes for man. Along the surf-beaten shores, and within the forest glades, where the streamlets coursed down their rocky beds, the rude colonists built their huts of heath and branches, and raised the grave-mounds over the remains of their distinguished heroes; whilst with their frail weapons of stone and flint, they struggled for existence with the fierce denizens of the woods.

We have no means of ascertaining how long the primitive Allophyliæ retained possession of the British Islands before the first wave of the great Celtic race broke upon our shores. Dr Wilson has associated the intrusion of the Celtæ with the introduction of the metallurgic arts; but the monuments of

many hundred specimens there assembled bear the plainest traces of human skill, and are genuine vouchers of the existence of man in the age of the fossil elephant and other gigantic animals entombed in the Diluvium of Geologists."—*Blackwood's Magazine*, October, 1860.

the Stone Period were common to all primitive nations; and as, in the absence of more reliable data than the mere outward configuration and internal arrangement of the sepulchral mounds of Arran, it would be futile to attempt any indication of the period of their construction, or the people by whom they were built, we shall proceed to do little more than enumerate and describe these interesting monuments, and leave the enigma of their origin to be solved by more recondite and experienced archæologists.

CHAPTER II.

Barrows* and Cairns.†

"Green along the ocean's side,
  The mounds arise, where heroes died."

THE *tumuli* or mounds are probably the most primitive and universal of all the old sepulchral monuments. Their existence has been traced in almost every country of the known world—along the shores of Europe; within the steppes of Tartary and the wilds of Siberia; over the hunting-fields of North America, the prairies of Mexico, and the sunny plains of Africa; and within the forest ranges of South America and the jungles of Hindostan—indicating one common sentiment of the human mind, in its primeval barbarism, the passionate desire for sepulchral honours.

"If fall I must in the field," says Shilric, "raise high my grave, Vinvela. Gray stones and heaped-up earth shall mark me to future times. When the hunter shall sit by the mound, and produce his food at noon, 'Some warrior rests here,' he will say; and my name shall live in his praise."

---

* Barrow—beorh—bearw; hence to burrow.

† Cairn—Kærn—a heap of stones; Carnydd—Wales; Galgals—France.

The distinction between the Barrow and the Cairn consists in the former being composed entirely of earth, and the latter of stones, or stones and earth.

The hunting-ground and the battle-field were the arenas where the sepulchral honours were fought for and won by the ancients; death was the gateway, and the grave-mound the entrance-hall to the Walhalla—the Nirwana and the Elysium of the brave.

The magnitude of the funeral pile and the *tumulus* appears to have been proportioned in accordance with the rank and celebrity of the chief in whose honour they were raised. But the Greeks and Romans launched out into great extravagance in the time of Alexander in the dimensions and magnificence of their sepulchral monuments. Several laws were made at Athens to restrain the vanity of the Greek *tumuli* builders. Plato proposed a regulation, that no mound should be larger than what five men could complete in five days, nor a pillar higher than would contain four heroic verses.

The "Adventures of Beowulf," an old Anglo-Saxon poem, contains the description of the pile and mound raised by the Saxons in honour of their deceased leader. The pile for the burning of the body was

"Hung round with helmets,
With boards of war,*
And with bright byrnies,†
As he had requested.
Then the heroes weeping,
Laid down in the midst
The famous chieftain—
Their dear lord.
Then began on the hill
The warriors to awake
The mightiest funeral fires;

* Shields. † Coats of mail.

The wood smoke rose aloft,
Dark from the fire;
Noisily it went
Mingled with weeping."

After the burning of the body, they proceeded to raise

"A mound over the sea—
It was high and broad—
By the sailors, over the waves,
To be seen afar.
And they built up
During ten days
The beacon of the war renowned.
They surrounded it with a wall,
In the most honourable manner
That wise men could devise.
They put into the mound
Rings and bright gems,
All such ornaments."*

Mr R. C. Hoare, who has acquired, by long and careful examination, an intimate knowledge of the *tumuli* of the British
Isles, has suggested for these monuments the following
classification, based chiefly upon the peculiar characteristics
of their configuration:—The Long Barrow; the Bowl Barrow; the Conoid Barrow; the Druid Barrow; the Eucircled
Barrow; the Enclosed Barrow, etc.

This system of classification applies with equal pertinence
to the cairns or stone *tumuli*, which, on account of the lapi-
dose nature of the surface soil, predominate throughout the
Highlands of Scotland and the Western Islands.

The only specimens of the barrow, or earthen *tumulus*,

---

* "The Celt, the Roman, and the Saxon."

which have been discovered in Arran are a group, which at
one time existed in Glen Cloy, near Brodick Bay. One of
these mounds was depressed or hollowed on the top, and
another was capped by a circle of stones "whose ends just
appeared above the earth."* The former represents the
Bowl Barrow, which is frequently to be met with in the
Hebrides.† The latter is of rare occurrence in the British
Isles, but prevails throughout the north of Europe.

The most interesting and numerous of the Stone *Tumuli*,
which we have observed in Arran, are the CHAMBERED
CAIRNS, consisting of a series of cells or chambers of huge
unwrought slabs, containing human bones or cinerary urns.
Cairns of this class are common in Ireland, and are identical
in formation with the *Jættestuer*, or Giant's Graves of Scandinavia. An investigation of their contents has disclosed the
rude flint and stone weapons and ornaments of the Stone
Period, beside the crumbling bones or inurned ashes of the
dead—referring to a period prior to the introduction of
metals, and contemporaneous with the rites of the funeral pile.

In Mauchrie Moor there may still be seen the inner trough
or chamber of a denuded cairn, formed by four huge stones,
beneath which a large heap of flint flakes and arrow-heads
was lately dug up. In the same moor, forests of oak lie
crumbling amid the heath and moss, which half conceal the
grave mounds of the ancient islanders.

It has been conjectured that these monuments have been

---

* Pennant. Vol. III., p. 210.

† About 2000 barrows of this description have been found in the
Orkney Islands.—*Wilson's Archæology*, p. 55.

used from generation to generation as the burial vaults of
families or tribes; but such an hypothesis appears untenable
when we consider the improvident habits of the early *tumuli*
builders, and the exclusive use of the cairn as a monument
for the brave and distinguished dead. It is more probable
that many of these cairns may have been raised on the battle-
field after some fierce intestine feud or foreign invasion.
The confused and huddled appearance of the bones in the
rude cells or catacombs confirms this opinion. In several of
the chambered cairns which have been opened in England,
the intersecting passage which divides the cells has been
found strewn with bones, as if carelessly dropt whilst being
hastily interred in the grave trough. The traditions too
which float around this class of the Arran grave mounds
are associated with the fierce raids and clanish feuds of early
times; and it is said that the ghosts of the buried dead were
wont to rise from their graves and renew the combat in the
shadowy folds of the evening mists.

On the farm of Blairmore, near the base of Dunfiun, may
be seen the scattered ruins of a chambered cairn.* On the
stones being carried away some years ago, to build the Lamlash school-house, a series of inner cells was exposed, each
covered with a single flat stone.

At Torlin, on a green bank near the shore, there is an
interesting specimen of the "elongated" chambered cairn. It
is intersected from east to west by a row of vaults, consisting
each of six unhewn slabs, from five to eight feet square.
These vaults or chambers were filled with human bones,

* Pennant. Vol. II., p. 212.

some of which, we were informed, were cleft as if from the blow of an axe or hatchet. This cairn was partially removed some years ago by a modern Goth, who rifled the cells of their contents, and strewed them over his field. With daring irreverence, he selected one of the largest skulls from the ghastly heap, and carried it home with him; but scarcely had he entered his house when its walls were shaken as if struck by a tornado. Again and again the avenging blast swept over his dwelling, though not a sigh of the gentlest breeze was heard in the neighbouring wood. The affrighted victim hastened to re-bury the bones in their desecrated grave, but day and night shadowy phantoms continued to haunt his mind and track his steps, and a few months after the commission of his rash deed, whilst riding along the high road towards Lag, he was thrown from his horse over a steep embankment, and dashed against the rocks of the stream beneath.*

It was with some feelings of trepidation, after listening to this fearful tragedy, that we proceeded to remove the stones and earth which filled the rifled cells of this ghost-haunted cairn; but a few marine shells, mixed with the small delicate bones of birds, were all we could discover to repay our labour.†

* This tradition is well known in Arran, and has tended to deepen the feelings of superstitious dread with which these monuments are generally regarded.

† It is worthy of notice that in the barrows and giants' graves of Finland there have been found large quantities of the bones of birds and the skulls of small wild animals, suggestive of some old superstition, the origin and nature of which are concealed amongst the mysteries of the past. It is probable, however, that the ancient Celts, like the Gauls, drew their auguries from birds, as they hold a prominent place in many Highland traditions.

Some years ago a "white cairn," near Largiebeg, was denuded of its stones, exposing a range of chambers containing several rude urns of unbaked clay, filled with earth and calcined bones.

Near Dippen, on a little green knoll by the shore, there are the remains of a chambered cairn. The huge stone troughs appear to have been built irregularly near the centre of the mound.

Between the little straggling village of Shiskin and Auchingallan, there stretches along the coast a broad waste of unreclaimed moorland, studded by groups of cairns, monoliths, and stone circles. Near the southern extremity of the moor, within the lands of Torbeg—Little Hill—there may be seen the ruins of an interesting cairn, measuring about three hundred and fifty feet in circumference. It is intersected from north to south by a concentric row of chambers, each chamber consisting of five unhewn slabs of three to five feet in height.

Wandering northward, towards the Mauchrie Bay, through the tall heath and the mossy tarns, we arrive at Tormore— Great Hill—deriving its name probably from some gigantic *tumulus*, which may have appeared in olden times, like a natural eminence rising above the waveless moorland,[*] for neither hill nor mountain ridge breaks the monotony of the dreary expanse of moss and peat-bog, excepting here and there the rifled grave mounds or fallen monoliths of the buried dead. About a stone's-cast from the shore we per-

---

[*] On the farm of Tormore there is a cairn known by this name, but it appears to have but lately received the designation.

ceive the exposed cells of one of these cairns—huge slabs of red sandstone and granite, deeply sunk in the moss. Still farther north, on the farm of Auchingallan, there is a *tumulus* known as the "White Cairn."

Where the lovely Glen Cloy—Lewis—opens into the Bay of Lamlash, a few minutes' walk from the mansion house of the Fullerton family, there is a green mound, which was dug into some years ago. On removing the superincumbent earth and stones, a collection of small square chambers of flat unhewn slabs was discovered, from which were taken two rude clay urns of the primitive flower-pot pattern, containing calcined bones.

Another interesting class of the sepulchral mound is the ENCIRCLED CAIRN, so called from its being surrounded by a circle of upright stones. This description of *tumulus* is of common occurrence throughout the north of Europe, and apparently belongs to an antiquity less remote than that of the chambered cairn. From the identity of their outward configuration with the encircled barrows of Norway and Sweden, a Scandinavian origin has been assigned to those which exist in the British Islands; but an examination of their contents controverts this opinion, and refers their origin to the transitionary period of the metallurgic history, when the rude Britons were laboriously working the mines of Cornwall, and smelting and moulding the ores into weapons and instruments of bronze.

The Greeks and Romans, too, appear to have occasionally surmounted their sepulchral mounds with stone columns, and encompassed them with earthen vallums or stone

D

circles.*   The *tumulus* raised over the ashes of Patroclus,
belonged to this class:—

> "Designing next the compass of the tomb,
> They marked the boundary with stones, then filled
> The wide enclosure hastily with earth."†

It is probable, indeed, that many of the smaller stone
circles, which fling their mysterious shadows over the glens
and moors of the Highlands and Isles of Scotland, are but
the remains of encircled cairns rifled of their contents.   On a
green bank, near the shore at Mauchrie, there is a cairn about
one hundred and fifty feet in circumference, which has been
partly removed for the building of a neighbouring dyke, but
the huge stone columns which surround the mound are still
entire.   In a few years the stone circle, with its halo of
Druidic superstitions, may be the only relic of the encircled
tumulus.

In the neighbourhood of Tormore there is a cairn, noticed
by Pennant, within a concentric circle.‡

Near Corrie Crievie, to the south of the Preaching Cave,
there is an imperfect cairn, within three concentric circles.
Large rounded boulders from the passing stream form the interior mound.   There are the remains of a similar *tumulus,*
about two hundred feet in circumference, in the neighbourhood of Slidry.

* On the removal of an encircled *tumulus* in the neighbourhood of
Rutherglen, a series of cistvæns was discovered, containing amongst
other relics two brass vessels, upon the handles of which the Roman
name "Congallus," or "Convallus," was engraved.—*Wilson's Archæology,* p. 55.
                † Homer's Iliad.—*Cowper's Translation,* p. 420.
                    ‡ Pennant.   Vol. II., p. 206.

Another class of the sepulchral mounds of Arran is the
SHIP BARROW or CAIRN, analogous in design with the *Skibs-*
sœtninger of Sweden. These *tumuli* are described by Chalmers as "oblong ridges, like the hulk of a ship with its bottom
upwards." From the Norse sagas we learn that it was an
old custom to bury the daring sea Vikings beneath a barrow
or cairn, constructed in the form of a ship, and occasionally
the long dark galley itself, which had rode many a stormy
sea, was dragged ashore to cover the ashes of its brave com-
mander.

There is an interesting example of the ship barrow, in the
mound of Saint Columba, within the little haven of Churaich
—Port-a-Curragh* in Iona. It is about fifty feet in length,
and is said to have been built after the model of the rude
currach of wicker and hides, in which the Saint landed on the
island. A smaller ridge lies in juxtaposition to the large
mound, which is supposed to represent the little boat towed
astern.†

On the bank of the Slidry stream, to the south of Arran,
there is an elongated, ship-like cairn, exactly similar to the
celebrated *currach* mound of Iona. It is thirty feet in length,
with a smaller ridge attached, measuring nine feet. The sides
of the *tumuli* are trenched with flat, flag-like stones, and at
each end there stands a large monolith of red sandstone,
encrusted with lichen and moss. This monument is supposed
to mark the grave of one of Fion-gal's heroes, about whom
many strange stories are told. An anxious treasure-seeker,

---

* Port-a-Curragh—Bay of the Boat.
† Wilson's Archæology, p. 57.

who dug into the larger mound, is said to have found a huge
bone, into the hollow of which he thrust down his foot and
leg as into a boot.[*]

On the southern shoulder of one of the heath-clad hills
which buttress the entrance to Glen Ashdale, there is another
long ridge-like *tumulus*, with its smaller contiguous mound
and standing stones, known in the district as the "Giant's
Grave."

Dr Wilson has assigned the origin of these ship-like cairns
of Scotland, from their resemblance to the *Skibssœtninger* of
the North, to the time

"When Norse and Danish galleys plied
Their oars within the Frith of Clyde."[†]

But in the absence of more trustworthy evidence than the
mere analogy of construction, such an opinion must be received with caution. The crowned and encircled *tumuli* are
even more numerous in Norway and Sweden than the
Skibssœtninger, but they are also of common occurrence in
the British Isles, and, as we have seen, were in use amongst
the Greeks and Romans. Many a brave Viking found his
grave along the surf-beaten shores of the Western Isles, but
tradition alone now hovers over the mound where his ashes
sleep.

There are a few more *tumuli* in Arran worthy of notice,
though difficult of classification.

Near the base of the Ross Hills, where the Monie-mhor
Glen narrows into a bosky ravine, there may be traced the

* Headrick's Arran, p. 148.
† Wilson's Archæology, p. 57.

remains of a cairn which, when entire, is said to have measured about two hundred feet in circumference. On being partially removed some years ago, for the building of a neighbouring dike, several *cistvæns* or stone coffins were exposed, consisting of six unhewn flags, and containing human bones.*

On the banks of the Clachan Burnie—rill of stones—there is a circular cairn.

Pennant notices the existence of an elongated *tumulus* at Feorling, in Drumidoon Bay. It was built of rounded stones from the shore, and measured one hundred and fourteen feet in diameter.

Perhaps the largest cairn in Scotland, but of which scarcely a stone now remains, stood upon the shore at Blackwater-foot. It was of a circular, conoid formation, measuring two hundred feet across †—about twice the size of the tumulus raised over the ashes of Patroclus on the plains of Troy. Several thousand cart-loads of stones were removed from this cairn for the building of the rude cots of the fishermen which cluster at the mouth of the Blackwater, when large numbers of stone coffins were discovered, filled with human bones, placed irregularly over the surface soil, but not a vestige of stone or metallic implement could be found. The huge flag-stones of the cistvæns may still be seen, built into the dikes and houses, investing the little hamlet with the mysterious memorials and ghostly traditions of pre-historic times.

The cairn is not exclusively a sepulchral monument. Like

* New Statistical Account.
† Headrick; New Statistical Account, etc.

the monolith, it was frequently raised to commemorate some
civil compact, foreign raid, or clanish strife, and during the
times of feudal chieftainship, the heath-covered mound was
the primitive Justice Seat or *Tynwald* of the Highlands and
Isles.   A heap of stones was gathered on the field of Mizpah
to seal the covenant between Jacob and Laban;* and from
the time of Ezekiel to the present day, it has been the custom
in the East to mark the spot where a murder was committed
by a mound of stones.†   Laws were promulgated by the
early kings of Scotland from the coronation chair, "*super
montem de Scone.*"‡   Near Dun-tuilm Castle, there is a
hill known as Cnock-an-eirich—Hill of Pleas—from which
justice was dispensed in olden times.§   Thomas, the fourth
Lord of Lovat, held his court on the top of Tomnahwich.
These mounds were called, and in many parts of Scotland
are still known, as moats, laws, and court hills.‖

Near the celebrated stone circles on Mauchrie Moor, Arran,
there is a cairn, partly demolished, which Fion-gal, the hero
of Highland tradition, is said to have used as his justice-seat;
and the stone, beside which the culprit stood—a huge block
of red sandstone, is pointed out as the "Panel's Stone."

In Glen-in-tshuidhe there once stood a heath-clad mound

---

* Genesis xxxi. 45, 46.

† The Fidjee Islanders, as they wander through the dark forests of
their native glens, frequently turn aside to pluck a handful of leaves
to throw upon the spot where some warrior had been clubbed and
scalped.—*Willis' Travels.*

‡ Chalmers' Caledonia.   § Pennant.   Vol. III., p. 351.

‖ These were occasionally natural eminences, but more frequently
artificial.

of stones, called Suidhe Challum Chille—Saint Columba's Seat—where the Saint is believed to have sat and refreshed himself when weary with his walk through the dense forest glades of the island.

On the shore, near Catacol, there once stood a circular cairn, known as Aran*—Ar Fhinn—Slaughter of Fion-gal, said to have been raised to commemorate the invasion, defeat, and death of Manos, King of Sweden. An old Highland poem, which was wont to be chanted in the Isles by the ingle-nook, during the last century, contains the leading incidents of this episode in the traditional history of Arran. It appears that, on the defeat of his forces, Manos was disarmed and bound by Fion-gal, but on pledging his faith to return to his own country, and cease his predatory invasions of the Inisfail,† he was at once liberated by his generous conqueror. Scarcely had the Norse galleys, however, left the island, when Manos was induced by the entreaties of his men to return and renew the conflict. The sequel is thus graphically described towards the conclusion of the poem. We give the original and translation :—

> " 'Se comhairle thug na sloigh
> Ar Manos mòr, na long àigh
> Tighin chuig' ar an ais o'n chuan
> Go maithibh sluagh Innsefàil.
> Thill na laoich nan caogadaibh borb,
> Bu mhor an toirm ar an tràigh.
> Mar fhuaim tuinne bha gach treud,
> Is faram nan ceud ann ar dàil.

* Statistical Account.

† Inisfail—Innse nan Gall—Isles of the Strangers—a name given to the Hebrides.

Chuir Fionn teachdaire gu luath
Go Manos nan ruag is nan gniomh.
' Càite bheil do mhionna mòra
Fhir nach cum a choir ach cli.'
    Fhreagair an Triath gu fiata borb,
Ar am biodh colg anns gach greis,
' Fhàgas iad in deallt an fheoir
Ar an lòn ud siar ma dhcas.'
    Thug sinn an sin deannal cruaidh
Mar nach fac 's nach cuala mi.
Mar theirbeirt teine na nial.
Bha gach triath a sgatha sios.
Mar choille chriònaich ar ant shliabh
Is an osag dhian ann nan car,
B'amhlaidh slachdraich nan sonn
A tuiteam fui 'r bonn 'sa chath.
Thuit Manos, àrman an nan t sluaigh
Mar lèig theine an cuan na sruth,
B'aneibnin iolach nan laoich
Nu air a chualas gach taobh an guth.
Mach o fhear a dh'iarr a sìth
No ghabh a dhìdion fu'r sgèith,
Do chuideachd rìgh Lochlan gu fior
Cha deachai duine d'a thir fein.
Bheirimse briatha do m' rìgh
Riamh ann stri nach d'fhuiling tàir
Gu 'n do thuit do na seachd cathain
Trian do mhaithibh Innsefàil." *

TRANSLATION.

" The hosts offered an advice
    To the great Manos of successful ships,
    To trace back their way upon ocean,
    To meet the chiefs of the host of Inisphail.
    So the heroes returned by their fifties fierce,
    And loud was their noise on the strand.

* This poem occurs in the collection of Mr Duncan Kennedy, who was for some time resident in Glasgow. It is now in the possession of the Highland Society.—Report of Highland Society on Ossian's Poems, pp. 328-332.

Like a roaring wave each band advanced.
Fingal immediately despatched a messenger
To Manos of the victorious pursuits and exploits:
' Where are thy solemn oaths,
Thou man that upholdest faith but with thy left hand?'
Fierce and furious answered the chief,
With the wonted frown of his wrath,
' I left them on the dew of the grass,
In yonder meadow to the south-west.'
We then made the impetuous onset,
Such as I have not seen nor heard of.
As a cloud gives out its fire,
Each hero dealt destruction.
As the decayed grove of the mountain
Sinks under the rapid sweep of the whirlwind,
So were the mighty overturned
As they fell under our feet in battle.
Manos, leader of the host, has fallen,
Like a fiery meteor in the forth of currents.
Grievous was the cry of his heroes,
When their spreading voice was heard around.
    Except a man who sought his peace,
Or who took protection under our shield,
None of the followers of Lochlin's king
Returned to his own land.
    I declare by my king,
Who was never defeated in battle,
That there fell in our seven bands
A third of the chiefs of Inisfail."

This interesting memorial monument of Fingalian prowess, the Aran* cairn, was removed some years ago, and from its stones an excellent road has been made by the utilitarian Islanders.†

It was an ancient custom in Arran and throughout the

---

* From which some etymologists have derived the name of the Island.
† New Statistical Account.

E

Highlands to cover the spot with stones where the coffin was placed, on its way to the church-yard, whilst the weary mourners tarried by the road-side to refresh themselves. The old burial-place at Shiskin, on the west coast of Arran, was much revered by the natives, on account of its reputed consecration by Saint Molios; and many of the villagers of Lamlash were wont to bury their dead within the sacred enclosure of the Clachan, beside the traditional tombstone of the Saint. On their journey across the moors, the funeral attendants halted near the head of Monie-mhor Glen, where a huge cairn of stones, raised during successive generations, now marks the site where the encoffined dead was placed. *

Whilst wandering over the hills and the moors of the Island, we occasionally stumble against a little mound or cairn of stones but a few feet in circumference. Many of these tiny cairns, tapestried with heath and moss, are regarded by tradition as the graves of lawless caterans, who perished by the dirks of rival clansmen in the old feudal times. Such is supposed to have been the origin of a small green *tumulus* which was removed some years ago from a heathery knoll, beside the little white cots of the Cordon, to the south of Lamlash. It is said that an old sceptic to ghostly superstitions, in spite of warning and remonstrance, carried away the stones of the mound for the building of a house for himself and family; but though he toiled for days at the work, he could make no progress; some unseen agency

---

* Stat. Acct., Buteshire—Local Tradition. There is the *Hilloch Sweyne*—Mound of the Burden in Iona, on which bodies brought to the Bay of Martyrs were placed.

continued to demolish the walls as they were being built, and he was forced to relinquish the impious undertaking.

The meagre acquaintance which we possess of the contents of the Barrows and Cairns of Arran, has induced us to embrace these monuments generally within the Primeval or Stone Period; but though the sepulchral mound originated and obtained during the earliest times, it was likewise in common use during the later eras of pre-historic annals.

In some Eastern countries it was associated with dishonour and desecration: Achan for his sins was commanded to be stoned by Joshua; "and all Israel stoned him with stones; and they raised over him a great heap of stones unto this day."[*] During the dark ages of priestly domination in Britain, the heretic and the suicide, who died without the pale of the church, were occasionally condemned to pagan sepulture. The reference by Shakespere to the burial of the unfortunate Ophelia, is doubtless in allusion to this practice:

> "But," demurs the priest, "that great command o'er—sways the
> order,
> She should in ground unsanctified have lodg'd
> Till the last trumpet; for charitable prayers,
> Shards,[†] flints, and pebbles should be thrown on her."

But amongst the early Britons the *tumulus* was regarded as the most honourable monument of interment, and was reserved exclusively for the chiefs and distinguished heroes of the communities or tribes. After the introduction of Christianity, however, the barrow and the cairn, though still reverenced for their antiquity, were abhorred for their un-

---

[*] Joshua vii. 25, 26.   [†] Fragments of Pottery.

sanctity; and the old pagan mode of sepulture, with its cinerary rites and bardic elegies, was superseded by simple inhumation beneath the shadow of the Christian fane.

The deep-rooted attachment of the Highlanders to the old customs and practices of their forefathers, preserved the use of the cairn, amidst the Highland glens and Western Islands of Scotland, long after it was abandoned in the south. "*Curri mi clach er do cuirn*"—I will add a stone to your cairn—is a proverbial expression still in use in some parts of the Highlands. The sepulchral cairn, with its covering of velvet moss, tufted with fern and heath, which four thousand years ago was raised over the ashes of the distinguished warrior chief on the rocky shore of the Sudreyjar Islet, has its prototype in the little mound of pebbles, heaped over the grave of the humble islander in the clachan church-yard of Shiskin.

The plough-share of the native agriculturist has passed over the site of many of the *tumuli* of Arran; but the old grave mounds which still exist are regarded with feelings of superstitious reverence, and many a weird and wild tradition envelopes them with a mysterious and sacred protection.

CHAPTER III.

Cromlechs.

"Speak thou, whose massy strength and stature scorn
The power of years—pre-eminent and placed
Apart, to overlook the circle vast."

THE term Cromlech is derived from the Gaelic *cromadh*—a roof or vault, and *clach*—a stone.* It generally consists of three or four unhewn columns, capped by a huge block of stone, forming a recess or chamber underneath, within which were placed the bones or incinerated ashes of the dead.

The origin and design of these monuments are shrouded in the mists of the past, but their intimate association with the chambered cairn, one of the earliest monuments we possess of the ancient Britons, suggests their contemporiety with the earliest dawn of the pre-historic era, when the rude Allophyliæ were building their huts of wicker and turf along the shores of the British Islands.

Though of less frequent occurrence than the cairn or the monolith, their existence has been traced from the cradle-land of the human race, along the banks of the Jordan, to the sunny islets of the Mediterranean; over the European continent, and within the forest jungles of America.

---

* In France, the Cromlech, consisting of four stones, is called a *Dolmen;* three stones, a *Trilith;* and two stones, a *Semi-dolmen.*

The cromlech, like the stone circle, was long regarded by popular superstition as a relic of Druidism, and many of the inhabitants of the Highlands and Islands of Scotland, to the present day, believe that human sacrifices were offered by the Druid priest on its huge capstone, whilst the reeking blood of the victims flowed down into the little recess beneath. Modern investigation, however, has satisfactorily proved the sepulchral origin and design of these elaborate structures. They are occasionally found buried beneath the barrow and cairn, or enclosed within the stone circle; and from the little chamber of the *trilith* or *dolmen*, the crumbling bones of the brave hunter or warrior chief have been disentombed.

In 1825, a large cromlech, consisting of four stones, was exposed in removing a cairn on the neighbouring coast of Kintyre, and within the recess human bones were found, mingled with those of the horse and the cow.[*]

A little to the south of Druim-cruey, in Arran, there lately existed an interesting cromlech, enclosed within a stone circle. It consisted of a large flat block of red sandstone, supported by three lesser ones, and is described by Martin as an altar-piece, upon which the ancient inhabitants of the island were wont to burn their sacrifices in times of heathenism.[†]

Headrick refers to a remarkable specimen of the *trilith*, or cromlech of three stones. The copestone, of vast dimensions, is represented as resting on two smaller ledges, deeply sunk in the earth.[‡]

---

[*] Wilson's Archæology, p. 67.
[†] Martin's Western Islands, p. 220.
[‡] Headrick's Arran, p. 46.

It has been asserted that the erection of this class of monuments was confined exclusively to a period prior to the introduction of the funeral pile; but an examination of the
cromlechs of Arran has clearly evinced their association with
the rites of cremation. One of the most perfect *triliths* we
have anywhere seen, stands on the farm of Drumidoon, a
little to the north of Blackwaterfoot. It consists of a huge
block of red sandstone, resting upon two smaller ledges, and
enclosing an area or chamber of two feet square, neatly
trenched with small, thin flag-stones. This chamber was
dug into some years ago, and a rude, flower-pot-shaped urn
of unbaked clay discovered, containing incinerated bones.
The urn and its contents crumbled into dust on being exposed
to the atmosphere. Tradition relates that the daughter of
Ossian was buried here.*

The magnitude of this class of monuments, and the vast
labour necessary for their construction, have excited the
astonishment of every age, and invested them with the
prestige of a supernatural origin. The huge cromlechs of
Brittany, extending over an area of about eight miles, are the
"Herculean work of Cyclops." In France they are known as
"Faeries' Tables," and the little chambers beneath as "Faeries'
Grottos." In Scandinavia they were regarded as the abodes
of the gods, and, long after the introduction of Christianity,
received divine honours. It is still a popular belief in some
parts of Anjou, that these vast amorphous blocks were torn
from their native crags by the faeries, who carried them down

* New Statistical Account.

in their aprons, and reared them in circles and cromlechs over the grassy plains of the lowlands. A similar tradition accounts for an interesting trilith on Craigmadden Moor, Stirlingshire, the stones of which are of many tons' weight. "A narrow, triangular space remains open between the three stones, and through this every stranger is required to pass on first visiting the spot, if, according to the rustic creed, he would escape the calamity of dying childless."*

But the faerie mythology which surrounds the cromlechs of Arran is not less marvellous than that which floats about the *dolmens* and *triliths* of Anjou and Craigmadden Moor:— Once upon a time a bevy of faeries met on the summit of Durra-na-each, near Shiskin, and proceeded to amuse themselves by throwing down pebbles amongst the trees of the Mauchrie forest. The "rules of the game" required that the stones should be thrown from between the finger and the thumb. Many centuries have passed since then, and the giant oaks of the Mauchrie have crumbled into dust, but over the moor may still be seen the *pebbles* of the faeries in the gray monoliths and stone circles which lie buried in the moss and heath.

The primitive design of the cromlech has been preserved, by successive generations, from the earliest dawn of archæological history till the present time. In the rude cells or

---

* Wilson's Archæology, p. 66. The fair maids of Columbiers, in France, are still accustomed to climb upon the cromlech and leave a piece of money on its copestone, believing that the offering will provide them with husbands ere the year closes.— *Wright's Celt, Roman, and Saxon, p.* 63.

vaults of the chambered cairn; in the *cistvæns* or stone chests which have been disentombed from the British *tumuli;* and in the stone coffins and horizontal grave slabs, with their tiny supporting columns, of our country church-yards, we may trace the same peculiar constructive formation, conceived and designed by the old cromlech builders some thousands of years ago.

F

CHAPTER IV.

Single Monoliths or Standing Stones.

"Those lonely columns stand sublime,
Flinging their shadows from on high,
Like dials which the wizard, Time,
Had raised to count his ages by."—MOORE.

THE erection of stone columns, to distinguish the grave of the
hero chief; to mark the boundaries of lands; and to commemorate some civil compact, clanish feud, or foreign invasion; were customs common to all primitive nations.

These monuments are found in almost every glen and forest
glade and mossy waste of the Scottish Highlands and Western
Isles, but perhaps in no islet of the Hebrides are they so frequently to be met with as in the little Island of Arran. The
origin and design of their erection are now buried in the
secrets of the past. No rude inscription or hieroglyphic
symbol has been traced beneath the encrusting lichen and
moss; and no time-honoured record exists, to tell the story
of their builders.

Tradition has poured a flood of Fingalian romance over the
gray monoliths of Arran, and many a heart-stirring legend is
told of the heroes who fought and died on the Mauchrie
Moor, and who are now believed to lie buried beneath the
tall columns which were raised in honour of their prowess.

Standing Stone, Mauchrie Moor.

There are frequent references, both in sacred and profane history, to the ancient custom of raising the monolith over the grave of the honoured dead.   Beneath a pillar, Jacob buried his beloved Rachel; and Olaus Magnus informs us, that it was one of Woden's laws to raise the *"bauta stein"* over the graves of distinguished heroes.

Stone coffins and cinerary urns have been occasionally dug up from beside the Arran monoliths, and the frequent association of many of these monuments, with the grave mounds of the early Islanders, indicates the sepulchral design of their erection.   In the neighbourhood of the standing stones at Tormore, near Shiskin, stone coffins and urns have been found whilst removing the peat from the moor.   Towards the south side of Kilmichael river, there lately existed, if it does not still exist, a standing stone about fifteen feet high, and near its base was discovered a stone chest filled with human bones.*   The aged Ossian, wandering over the deserted wilds of Argyll, exclaims—

> "Thou seest on every hill the tombs
> Of those who helped the unhappy.
> Thou seest their stones have sunk
> Amidst the rank rustling grass of the vale.
> The heroes have made their bed in dust;
> And silence, like mist, is spread in Morven."†

Many of the monoliths of Arran are no doubt the relics of comparatively modern times.   A few centuries ago, the lands of the Island were divided amongst several petty chiefs or barons, and standing stones were raised as *landmarks* to define the boundaries of their possessions, and prevent the

---

* Martin's Western Islands.   † Ossian's Poems.

encroachments of neighbouring chiefs. The traditional reverence with which the landmarks were regarded, entrenched as
they are by the sacred commands of Scripture,* has preserved
many of them from the desecration of modern utilitarians,
and within the dells and over the heathery moors, these rude
parchments of the Island chiefs may still be seen, mutely
eloquent of the old feudal times. By the roadside between
Brodick and Lamlash, there stand three massive blocks of
red sandstone, which are said to mark the spot where the
lands of three of the old proprietors of Arran met.† They
had a curious custom for preserving the remembrance of these
landmarks, and which appears to have been common to the
Western Islanders:—"They lay a quantity of the ashes of
burnt wood in the ground, and put big stones above the sand;
and for conveying the knowledge of this to posterity, they
carry some boys from both villages next the boundary, and
there whip them soundly, which they will be sure to remember and tell to their children."‡

The *termini* of the Romans are synonomous with the
grandes lapides of our old chartularies. In the encounter
between the gods, the poet represents Pallas as having

> " With strong grasp upheaved
> A rugged stone, black, pond'rous from the plain,
> A *landmark*, fix'd by men of ancient times,
> Which hurling at the neck of stormy Mars,
> She smote him."§

---

* " Remove not the ancient landmarks which thy fathers have set."
—Prov. xxii. 28.
    † Local tradition.   ‡ Martin's Western Isles, page 114.
        § Homer's Iliad—*Cowper's Translation*, page 391.

The "Pictish Chronicle" describes the boundaries of the territories ceded to the Culdees by the Pictish King, as having extended "*a lapide in Apurfeirt usque ad lapidem juxta Cairfiul.*" "In King Malcolme's times," says an old Scotch chronicle,[*] "was the red crosse erected, with the King of England's image on the one side, and the King of Scotland's on the other. This stone crosse was a march or mark between the two realms, standing in the middle of Stan-moore." And the celebrated stone on the field of Bannockburn—

> " Whose granite hand,
> Held up the exulting banner of the Bruce,
> Which all the proud day laughed with glorious scorn
> Upon the baffled foes,"

is supposed to have defined the western boundary of the ancient chase, when the Scottish kings of old hunted the deer through the forests of the Highland borders.[†] The remembrance of the march stones, which used to surround the borough towns of Scotland, still lingers among us; as also, the good old custom of riding round the boundaries in civic pomp.

The standing stone was also associated in ancient times with the consecration of the newly-elected king or chief; and the covenant or engagement, made beside the rude monolith, was invested with the sacredness of the most solemn oath. Josiah made a covenant with God, and Abimelech and Adonijah were raised to the kingly office, "standing by a pillar as the

---

[*] Published in 1612.
[†] Wilson's Archæology, page 92.

manner was."* These pillars were designated *Kong-stolen*
by the Danes; and amongst the northern nations were used
till the end of the fourteenth century, in connection with the
coronation rites of their kings and princes.† In the Scottish
Highlands they are known as *taniste*‡ stones, the most remarkable example of which is the celebrated *Lia Fail*, or Stone of
Destiny, which forms part of the coronation chair at Westminster Abbey. The ancient Scottish chroniclers, identify
the *Lia Fail* with the stone which the patriarch Jacob used
as a pillow on the field of Luz. It is said to have been
brought over to Ireland in the days of Romulus; and for
many ages the Irish kings were crowned upon it. From
Ireland it was removed to Iona; thence to Scone; and thence
to Westminster Abbey by Edward I., where it now remains;§
but the old bardic saw still holds good:—

> "Except old seers do feign,
> And wizard wits be blind,
> The Scots in place must reign
> Where they this stone shall find."‖

The Lords of the Isles had their *taniste* stone in Islay. It
is described by Martin as " a big stone of seven feet square,
in which there was a deep impression to receive the feet of
M'Donald." Standing upon this stone, the newly elected chief

---

* 2 Kings xxiii. 3.   Joshua xxiv. 26.   1 Kings i. 9.
† Ericus was made King of Sweden in 1396, standing upon the
Kong-stolen.
‡ Tanaiste—Gael—a thane, or lord.
§ Wilson's Archæology, pages 97, 98.
‖ Ni fallat fatum, Scoti quocunque locatum, invenient lapidem
regnare tetentur ibidem.

was consecrated by the Bishop of Argyll, and received the allegiance of his vassals.

The memorial standing stones appear, too, to have been designed and recognised as the popular records of important historical events, in olden times. A stone column was raised on the field near Renfrew, where Somerled, "the mighty of the Isles," was slain; and a number of standing stones commemorate the defeat of Macbeth near Dunsinane.* These monuments are known in the Highlands and Isles as *catstanes*, from the British *cad*, or the Scoto-Irish *cath*, a battle. At Maryreach, in Arran, there is said to have existed a stone column, which, tradition relates, was raised in remembrance of a treaty, entered into between the Islanders and the Norsemen in the days of Fion-gal.† At Kingscross, on a hillock near the shore, there is a monolith which marks the spot from which King Robert the Bruce embarked for the Carrick coast; and in a neighbouring field, there is an unhewn block of sandstone, believed to be the sole relic of the rude cot in which the king resided, on the eve of his departure from the Island.

Ossian beautifully and touchingly describes the feelings of veneration with which the memorial stones were regarded in early times. After the conflict between the forces of Cuthon and Fion-gal, a peace was declared between the chiefs, and the aged Lugar seizes the opportunity of addressing the two armies, as they are about to retire in friendship from the field:—

* Chalmers' Caledonia. Vol. I., pages 409, 410.
† Local tradition.

"Why," he said, "should they who go together to the
feast, meet in battle any more? Raise this
gray stone, the daughter of the rock, on the heath
of Moruth. The children of the years to come
shall mark it. They will ask the aged
warrior what it means. 'Lead me,' he will say,
'to the place.' With short, equal steps they walk
beside him. The blunt spear supports his
hand, and his gray dog, blind with years,
attends his steps. He hath reached the place;
he hath felt with joy the stone. 'It is,' he cries,
'the stone of Moruth.' 'Here,' leaning to it
his weary back, he adds, 'here your fathers
met in peace; they laid their hands together
to rear this gray stone. Forget not, children,
the peace of your fathers; remember it when
you behold the stone of Moruth!' Speak,
O stone! to the years that wander beyond the sun;
. . . . tell them, and the children who shall behold
them, that here we bade the battle cease. Let
the moss of years cover thee, thou sign of peace
on Moruth; let the ghosts of the dead defend thee;
let no unfriendly hand, no stormy blast, come nigh thee." *

The standing stones are more numerous in Arran along the
shores, where the ocean waves break in ceaseless surge against
the pebbly beach or the rocky cliff. Their sides are scarred
and seamed by the rains and snows of untold centuries; but
the fingers of Time have filled in the lines and wrinkles of
age, with hoary moss and emerald lichen; and now they

"Look like Druids of
Old with voices sad
And prophetic, —
Stand like hoar with
Beards that rest on
Their bosoms." †

* Smith's Translations of "Cathon."   + Longfellow's Hiawatha.

Concentric Stone Circle, Machrie Moor.

CHAPTER V.

Stone Circles.

"The hoary rocks of giant size,
That o'er the land in circles rise,
Of which tradition may not tell—
Fit circles for the wizard's spell;
Seen far amidst the scowling storm,
Seem each a tall and phantom form,
As hurrying vapours o'er them flee,
Frowning in grim security,
While, like a dread voice from the past,
Around them moans the autumnal blast."—MALCOLM.

THE stone circle has been found in almost every country where traces of the barrow or the cairn have been discovered.

Numerous hypotheses have been advanced to account for the origin and design of these mysterious monuments. The devotees of Druidism and Odinism have expended much useless learning in support of their respective theories, but they have either ignored or disregarded the only source of information from which, in the absence of historical evidence, trustworthy *data* could be derived; and not until comparatively recent times were investigations made, beneath or around the monuments themselves, with the view of ascertaining the antiquity or design of their construction.

The old Druid theosophy, still lingers among us. The stone circle is popularly regarded as the Druidic temple, and the cromlech as the altar, whereon the Druidic priest offered human sacrifices, under cover of the sacred grove—though indisputable evidence exists to justify the conclusion, that many of the rude columnar circles and cromlech altars owe their origin to the time when the primitive Allophylian, armed with his rude weapons of stone or flint, was struggling with the fierce carnivora of the Caledonian forests.

An interesting group of stone circles may be seen in the Mauchrie Moor, near the farm of Tormore, in Arran. Tradition relates that Fion-gal and his heroes were hunting the boar in the woods of the neighbouring glens, when a fleet of Norse galleys was seen approaching the shore. Scarcely had the marauders succeeded in effecting a landing in the Mauchrie Bay, when they were attacked by Fion-gal and his followers, and driven back to their ships. A few of the Vikings whose retreat had been cut off were chased over the Island, overtaken and slain near the old fort of Dunfiun — Fion-gal's fort. The Fingalian heroes who fell in the conflict were buried in the moor where they fought and died, and the huge stone columns, now half-concealed amid the tall heath, were raised in circles around their graves to the mournful song of the bards.*

The Mauchrie group consists of eight circles, all more or less complete, running irregularly from east to west; each circle comprising four to fourteen columns of rude unhewn sandstone, measuring three to eighteen feet in height, with an average circumference of eight feet. The diameters of the enclosed areas range from fifteen to thirty feet.

* Local tradition.

On entering the moor from the Shiskin road, we wander, in a north-westerly direction, through deep tufts of heath, tiny tarns, and peat-bogs, and in a few minutes arrive at the *first* of these circles. It consists of eight granite columns, three to four feet in height, with an areal diameter of twenty-seven feet.

The *second* circle is incomplete. It consists of three huge columns of red sandstone—the largest eighteen feet in height, and two smaller stones, deeply sunk in the moss; diameter of area, thirty feet.

The *third* consists of six stones, forming three-fourths of a circle; areal diameter, thirty feet.

The *fourth* measures fifteen feet across; and consists of six stones, averaging three feet in height.

The *fifth* is an interesting specimen of a *concentric* circle. The inner circle consists of eight stones three to four feet in height; the outer of fourteen stones of similar dimensions. Diameter of area, twenty-seven feet. This monument is known as *Suidhe-choir-Fhionn*, or, Fion-gal's Cauldron Seat.

The *sixth* consists of an erect column about twelve feet in height, with others just visible above the moss.

The *seventh* consists of two erect stones, four to six feet in height; the others are deeply imbedded in the moss.

The *eighth* is an imperfect circle, about twenty-nine feet in diameter. The stones are scattered and partially removed.

A careful examination of these and of similar monuments in Arran, has convinced us of the sepulchral origin and design of their construction. On removing the moss and heath which clad the area of the concentric circle above noticed, large stones and boulders were exposed, which we succeeded in removing to the depth of three to four feet, but without arriving at the original soil. Farther investigation convinced us that these stones had been placed there, at some remote antiquity, not beneath, but over the surface soil, and that during many centuries, the forests which covered the moor* had grown up and decayed around them, until the tiny cairn became entombed beneath the peat and the moss, and the tops of the tall columns alone appeared above the surface, to distinguish the grave of the ancient warrior chief.†

Human bones, urns, and stone chests are occasionally dug up in the neighbourhood of these circles; and the same indications of a sepulchral origin have been traced in connection with many of the encircled monuments of the Highlands of Scotland. Excavations were recently made in several small stone circles near the hills of Tuack in Aberdeenshire. In the centre of one of them, a cairn was discovered, from which a skull and bones were disinterred; and near the base of one of the columns, a hammer or axe-head of stone was found, placed over a heap of burnt bones. Urns filled with incine-

---

* The roots and trunks of oak trees are still found imbedded in the moss.

† Whilst the preceding pages were passing through the press, excavations were being made within the Tormore circles, by order and at the expense of his Grace the Duke of Hamilton.

The result has fully confirmed the opinion we have above expressed respecting the sepulchral design of these monuments. A stone coffin containing a skull, and two rude cinerary urns containing calcined bones, were discovered; and beside the remains of the distinguished native chiefs, were a few tiny arrow-heads, the frail weapons of the chase or the battle-field.

rated ashes, and fragments of bronze, were dug up from the base of two of the stones of an adjoining circle.

Whilst these discoveries tend to establish the sepulchral origin of the stone circle, they likewise prove the contemporiety of this class of monuments with the two earliest periods of the archæological annals; when the Allophylian and Celtic races were slowly emerging from their gross ignorance and barbarism, into a knowledge of the metallurgic arts, and the weapons of bronze were gradually superseding the hatchet, the spear, and the arrow-head of stone and flint.

It is by no means improbable that the peculiar construction of these monuments, in its adaptation to a sepulchral design, originated in the custom which existed amongst many early nations, of raising around the grave of the buried chief, as many stones as he had slain of the foe in the field of battle.[*] According to Boece, King Reutha—who is said to have lived about two centuries before the Christian era—"was the first king amang the Scottis, that fand imagine, to put nobill men for their vailyeant dedes in memory, and maid rich sepulturis for the bodyis of thaim that war slaine be Britonis, in defence of this realme. He commandit also monie hie stanis *to be set about the sepulture* of every nobill man as was slain be him of Britonis. In memory heirof, sindry of thaim remanis yet in the hielands, that the pepill may knaw sic men were vailyeant in thair dayis; throw quhilk, it came in use that the sepulturis of nobill men, was holdin in great reverence amang the people."[†]

* Wormii Monum. Dan. Pages 62, 63.
† Croniklis of Scotland. The Secund Buke, cap. x.

Ossian, too, indicates the custom of surrounding the buried hero with the memorial stones of his slaughtered foes, when he gives expression to the last wish of the dying Foldath: "Raise the tombs of those I have slain *around* my narrow house; often shall I forsake the blast to rejoice over their graves, when I behold them spread around with the long whistling grass."*

Much of the uncertainty and obscurity which surround the origin of the stone circles may have been occasioned by the error into which many writers have fallen, of mistaking the purposes to which such monuments were applied in succeeding ages, for the original design of their construction. When Time had invested it with the sacredness of antiquity, the stone circle was chosen, in many countries, as the council hall, or assembly chamber, where the sages and chiefs held their meetings, enacted laws, and dispensed justice, during the early historic ages. The shield forged by Vulcan for Achilles, bore amongst other devices, the representation of the "elders" sitting within the stone circle, and awarding justice to the plebeian throng—

> " On rough hewn stones, within the sacred cirque
> Convok'd, the hoary sages sat."†

And within the revered circle, by the side of the heathery hill, or in some bosky dell—where the mountain stream murmured its music beneath the drooping foliage of the brushwood—the Highland or Island chieftain, surrounded by armed retainers, held his law court in the old feudal times.

* Ossian's Poems.
† Homer's Iliad.—*Cowper's Translation*, page 348.

The stone circle was the justice-hall of the Orkney and Shetland Islanders until a very recent period, and it is still known in some districts by the name of the "Law-Ting." The chartulary of Moray contains the record of a regality court held by Alexander Stewart, Lord of Badenoch, son of Robert II., at the standing stones of Raitts, now Bellville,— "*apud le standand stanes de la Rath de Kingusy;*" and when the Bishop of Moray attended the court to protest against certain infringements of the rights of the Church, he stood "*extra circum.*"

The comparatively tiny sepulchral stone circles of the Highlands and Isles may have furnished the plan to later monolith builders for the construction of the vast monolithic monuments of Avebury, Stonehenge, and Stennis, the origin of which still remains a subject for the theories of the antiquary.

In one of the stones of Fion-gal's cauldron seat—Suidhe choir Fhionn—there is a remarkable perforation, which was probably associated with some old superstition or religious ceremony, now forgotten. The hole is sufficiently large to admit the two fingers, and runs perpendicularly through the side of the column. Tradition relates that to this stone Fion-gal was wont to tie his favourite dog Bran.*

The perforated columns are now of very rare occurrence in the British Isles, but it is probable that many of them have

---

* " Before the leash was prepared for him,
  Bran, though but a whelp,
  Killed a deer more than each of the rest."
  —*Ossian's Poems.*

been demolished on account of the heathen practices with which, even in comparatively modern times, they were connected, and to which frequent reference is made in the old Anglo-Saxon laws.* The Orcadian stone of Odin, situated near the Stennis circle, is a notable example of the perforated monolith. Lovers were wont to plight their troth standing beside it, by joining hands through the circular hole, and making the *promise of Odin;*† but even this old custom may be the relic of some older and grosser superstition, drifted down by tradition from the wreck of pagan mythology.

We have never witnessed a wilder and more grandly solemn scene than these old circles on the Mauchrie Moor, looming in the shadowy indistinctness of an autumn moonlight. The silence and solitude were unbroken, save by the whir of the startled moor-fowl among the tall heath, and the mournful dirge of the waves on the neighbouring beach. Scattered around were the rifled cairns and gray monoliths swathed in the evening mists, which crept along the hills and over the moorland waste. The shimmering moonbeams glistened like spectral lights on the tiny tarns, and flashed a silvery track across the dark channel of Kilbrannan. As we wandered amongst the old ruins, the weirdly stirring legends of the past haunted our mind, till the wreaths of mist seemed to float about like shadowy phantoms, and the circling monoliths and hoary cromlech appeared to rise from the heath,

---

* Mr Wilford, in his "Asiatic Researches," takes notice of the existence of perforated stones in some parts of India.

† Wilson's Archæology, p. 100.

like ghosts of the heroes of old, bending around the grave of their buried chief.

Many of the stone circles of Arran have been removed to make way for the advance of agriculture. A concentric circle on the farm of South Sannox was demolished a few years ago for the building of a dike; and a very complete single circle, which stood near the mouth of Glen Shirrag, was cleared away in preparing the field for the operations of the plough. But many of these monuments are still found in the Island, nestling amid the heath and brushwood of the glens, or rising from the grassy knolls around the coast. There is an interesting *gray* circle, surmounting a green mound, at Moniquil; and others may be seen at Mayish, Blaremore, Largiemore, Largiebeg, and other places.

CHAPTER VI.

Urns and Stone-Chests.

" A little urn—a little dust inside,'
Which once out-balanced the large earth, albeit,
To-day a four-years' child might carry it!"
E. B. BARRETT.

BESIDES the monuments which we have already described, and which appear to have been reserved for the great and the illustrious dead, *cistvœns* and cinerary urns are yearly dug up from the moors and the hills of Arran, undistinguished by super-incumbent cairn or barrow. In a field near Largiebeg, there existed a large collection of stone-chests, some buried a little below, and others partially appearing above the surface soil. This was probably a common burying-place of the early Islanders, or of some petty tribe, whose wicker huts clustered around the Whiting Bay. All traces of these old graves are now removed—the ploughshare of some daring Vandal passed over the field; and we were told that the upturned bones lay for many months scattered around; over which the ghosts of the desecrated dead wandered by night amid fitful gleams of lurid light!

The cists or stone-chests of Arran are of the simplest and rudest description. They consist generally of six unhewn slabs about six feet in length and two feet in breadth. They occasionally enclose the cinerary urn, but more frequently the calcined bones of the dead. Ou the farm of Blaremore, there was dug up some years ago a cist about four feet in length, containing a skeleton placed in a crouching position, as if in readiness to start up on the first summons of the war-cry. Arrow and spear-heads of stone and flint are frequently found beside the rude tenement of the buried chief, as if to supply his wants in the chase, when he rises to the aerial halls of his fathers.

It is probable that simple inhumation was the most ancient mode of interment, but the antiquity of the funeral pyre among primitive nations is proved from the association of calcined remains with the earliest sepulchral monuments of the archæological stone period. The causes which led to the origin and prevalence of the cinerary rites, may have been the desire to preserve the bodies of the deceased from the desecration of enemies, and from the mutilating attacks of the wild beasts which prowled amid the primeval forests of the old world. 'The body of Cornelius Sylla was burned by his friends to save it from the malice of his foes; and the body of Saul was reduced to ashes apparently from the same reason.

The adoption of urn-burial in the British Isles appears immediately to have followed the introduction of the funeral pyre, though it by no means superseded the more ancient mode of disposing of the dead by simple interment; and the frequent association of the urn and *cistvæn* beneath the same cairn, proves the contemporiety of cremation with simple inhumation, and the equal respect with which these customs were regarded by the early Britons. Amongst the Greeks

and Romans, urn-burial for a time prevailed, with all the
costly extravagance which characterised their sepulchral
tumuli and sculptured pillars. Their urns were of copper,
gold, or porphyry, according to the rank of the deceased.
Frequently large family urns were used, which received a
part of the ashes of every deceased member, whilst smaller
ones contained the collateral remains. The ashes of Domi-
tian were mingled with those of Julia, and of Achilles with
those of Patroclus.

The practice of cremation obtained throughout the countries of Northern Europe for several centuries after the
Christian era. There are records of its existence among the
Scandinavians till the latter part of the ninth century; and
during the thirteenth century, the Prussians are known to
have burned their dead on the funeral pyre. We have reason
to believe that the cinerary rites prevailed in North Britain
until the diffusion of Christianity, when they were abandoned for simple inhumation within the precincts of the
Christian church. In the days of Ninucius, the Christians
were denounced for their repression of cremation:—"*Exe-
crantur rogos et damnant ignium sepulturam.*"*

The earliest sepulchral monuments of Arran—the cairn,
the cromlech, and the monolith — are associated with the
cinerary urn; and it is probable that the custom of burning
the body prevailed during the Stone, Bronze, and Iron
Periods of the Island's history. A cist, containing a rude
clay urn of the flower-pot shape, was dug up from the farm

* On the relapse of the Esthonians to paganism in 1225, they disinterred their dead, and burned them on the funeral pyre.

of Arranton a few years ago; and, in the same neighbourhood, a large stone jar, containing earth and cinerary ashes,
was found, unaccompanied by the stone-chest. Similar relics
of primitive art have been discovered beneath the moss in
Glen Kill and other parts of the Island, besides those already
noticed in connection with the cairns of Glen Cloy and Largiebeg. The rude, inornate type of these vessels assigns their
origin to a period in the annals of Arran when the Islanders
were yet unskilled in the knowledge of the manipulative arts.

The ornate urns are probably the relics of a later period
and a more advanced civilisation. They are generally associated with metallurgic remains, and possess, in the design of
their ornamentation, a striking resemblance to the coarse
knitted fabrics occasionally exhumed from the British *tumuli*.
Whilst some workmen were engaged, about three years ago,
in digging the foundation for the new village of Glen Cloy,
a stone-chest and an urn of sun-baked clay, containing dust
and calcined human bones, were exposed, about two feet from
the surface soil. The latter was about eighteen inches in
height, and exhibited some degree of artistic skill in its ornamentation. Markings of the herring-bone pattern extended
down the neck; whilst the centre of the vessel, which bulged
out considerably, was surrounded at regular intervals by small
raised knobs.* An urn of similar type was found a few years
ago beneath the moss of the Mauchrie Moor. In shape, it
bulged out abruptly beneath the neck, tapering gradually
towards the bottom, and was adorned round the centre by an
alternation of horizontal and herring-bone markings.

* Letter by Dr Jamieson in *Glasgow Herald*.

CHAPTER VII.

"Behold yon huge
And unhewn sphere of living adamant,
Which, poised by magic, rests its central weight
On yonder pointed rock; firm as it seems,
Such is its strange and virtuous property,
It moves obsequious to the gentlest touch
Of him whose heart is pure; but to a traitor,
Though even a giant's prowess moved his arm,
It stands as firm as Snowdon."—MASON.

THE rudely primitive construction of the early pre-historic monuments, has led the over-zealous advocates of geology to class many of them amongst the freaks or accidents of natural causation. The sepulchral cairn is occasionally mistaken for the *morain* drifted by floating icebergs from the North, and deposited within the glens and along the straths of our Island. The unhewn columns and cromlechs, we are told, have been riven from their native crags by some convulsive throe of Nature, and now lie imbedded amidst the heath of the moorlands, to puzzle the antiquarian and excite the superstition of the credulous; and so also the rocking stone has been classed amongst the marvellous ingenuities of natural phenomena.

But the superstitious veneration with which the *logan*

stones have been regarded in every age, and in every country where they exist; their frequent association and occasional *connection* with the sepulchral cairns and monoliths;* and the unmistakeable existence of artificial construction which they exhibit, appear to us to furnish abundant evidence that these ponderous and ingeniously contrived monuments are the works of human design and labour.

An interesting specimen of the rocking stone may be seen near the shore at South Sannox, Arran. It consists of a rounded mass of granite resting upon a narrow ledge of pudding stone. Mr Headrick, who was less of an antiquarian than a geologist, thus refers to it:—"It is hardly credible that this stone could have rolled into its present position by accident. Its resting on a pivot, and having its edge propped by a small block of granite, seems to indicate that it was placed there by design. It very much resembles the rocking stones of Glen Nevis and other parts of the North Highlands."

The most convincing proof of the artificial construction of these monuments rests in their intimate association with the cairns, the cromlechs, and the stone circles—*a connection strongly suggestive of their sepulchral design.* Mr Akerman mentions that the famous Agglestone Barrow, in the Island of Purbeck, was surmounted by a rocking stone. And Appollonius Rhodius adds his testimony not only to the human contrivance of one of these monuments, but to its

* The logan stones of Perthshire are reared amongst the sepulchral monuments of the early Britons.—See Statistical Account, Wilson's Archæology, Borlase's Cornwall, etc.

design in increasing the distinction and celebrity of the sepulchral *tumulus:*—

> " In Tenos, by the blue waves compass'd round—
> High o'er the slain he heaped a funeral mound;
> Then rear'd two stones, to mark that sacred ground,
> One pois'd so light, that—as the mariner sees
> With wondering gaze—it stirs at every breeze."

The rocking stone has been found in England, Scotland, and Ireland, on the continent of Europe, and in several countries of the East. Pliny informs us that, at Harpasa, a town of Asia, there was "a rock of a wonderful nature; lay one finger to it and it will stir, but thrust at it with your whole body and it will not move." Ptolemy Hephestion also refers to the Gygonian Stone, near the ocean, which "may be moved by the stalk of an asphodel, but cannot be moved by any force." Among the Phœnicians they were known as Bætyli, or animated stones, and held sacred by them.

After the introduction of Christianity the rocking stones were designated the *Clacha-brath*, or stones of judgment; and it was believed that, so soon as these ponderous masses should wear through the pivots upon which they rested, the world would come to an end. For some years they were kept in constant motion by those who, like good Dr Cumming, were impatient for the consummation of terrestrial things; but the judgment stones have now grown rusty on their pivots, and many of them have been overturned by time-serving world-lings, who had little sympathy with the anxious zeal of their millenarian brethren.

The magnitude of the primitive amorphous monuments of

the stone period, and the vast labour which the early Britons must have employed in their construction, have contributed to deepen the feelings of veneration with which the mystery of their origin has, in every age, invested them.   The reverend statist of Kilmorie, in describing the stone circles of Mauchrie Moor, remarks:—"They consist of primitive red sandstone and millstone grit, a species of rock that is not to be found, *in situ*, near the spot.   They must, therefore, have been carried from a considerable distance, up a long but gentle ascent, to their present position.   The conveyance of such immense blocks from such a distance, and by such a way, would require more skill in mechanics than is possessed by the present inhabitants of the parish."*

The universality of the monolithic monuments appears to evince the existence of a common sentiment of the human mind in its primeval barbarism.   The rude Allophylian, whether amidst the old forests of the European Continent, or within the sea-girt islets of the Hebrides, must have oftentimes gazed with feelings of mingled fear and veneration on the sublime grandeur of Nature's works.   The dense, dark forests—the lofty mountains, with their serrated peaks—the storm, with the lightning's flash—and the surging sea, breaking in foam against the rocky coasts—filled his mind with an overwhelming sense of the existence of certain mysterious powers or divinities which governed the universe and overlooked the actions of man.   Hence the Pantheistic, Polytheistic, and Mythological systems, which, in one phase or other,

* New Statistical Account.

I

have formed the creed of all early nations. The weapons of
stone and flint, and other relics, found in the grave mounds
of the early Allophylian and Celtic races, prove their recog-
nition of, and belief in, a future existence; and in the daring
deeds and bravery of their lives, and the huge monuments
raised over their graves, we may discover the expression of
their homage and devotion to those sublime agencies of
creative power, by which their minds were impressed and
moulded.

The honour and reverence with which the monoliths and
cairns were invested by their builders, were increased in after
times by the mystic and shadowy remoteness of their antiquity, and the feelings which may have led to their erection
were revived and expressed in the superstitious stone worship
which prevailed in the East, and over the countries of the
European Continent, centuries after the Christian era. Till
the eleventh century, the laws of the Anglo-Saxons continued
to denounce and prohibit the worship of stones and rocks.*
The Scandinavians believed that a fairy or demon, whom they
were bound to propitiate, resided within the *Bauta-stein;*
and, during the last century, the inhabitants of the Western
Isles were wont to walk round the cairns and stone circles
from east to west,† as a mark of silent devotion. In the
parish of Dunlop there is a large stone, known as " Thugirt
Stone "—thou great stone—which was worshipped on bended
knee by the devotees of popery; and a few years ago the

---

* Pelgrave's Rise and Progress of the Celtic Commonwealth.
† Called *Deas-iul*, or way of the South.

monoliths of Ireland were the objects of the most grovelling idolatry.

The superstitions of the Arran people are deeply imbued with the legends of fairy mythology. The perforated column of "Fion-gal's Cauldron Seat," on the Mauchrie Moor, was believed to contain a fairy or brownie, who could only be propitiated by the pouring of milk through the hole bored in the side of the stone. The wife of Bath gossipp'd of the "old days of King Artour," when "all was this lond fulfilled of faerie," and adds—

> " I speke of many hundred yeres ago,
> But now can no man see none elves mo."

In Arran, however, the belief in fairies still lingers in the minds of the older inhabitants, and many curious stories are told of the pilfering habits and cunning tricks of the *wee-folks*, who held their midnight meetings within the stone circles and old forts of the Island.

Many of the minor relics of the stone period have been found beneath the moss and heath of the Arran glens and hills, but few of them have been deemed worthy of preservation. Arrow-heads of stone and flint are frequently picked up by the natives whilst digging peat in the moors. These instruments are generally about one to two inches in length, chipped or polished, and cut into the form of the primitive heart-shaped type; but more frequently they are *tanged* between the barbs, for fastening into the cleft shaft. They are called *elf-shots* by the Islanders, and are supposed to have been used by the fairies long ago.*

A beautifully polished spear-head, of fine granite, was found some years ago in the peat of the Monie-mhor Glen, also a stone hammer, about seven inches in length, pointed at the ends, and grooved in the centre to receive the handle. The stone hammers found in the grave mounds of the British Isles are of various forms and sizes, and must have cost the native artists much labour to chip and fashion into the required shape with the frail implements at their command. "As we find the little flint arrow-head associated with Scottish folk-lore as the *elfin's-bolt*, so the stone hammer of the same period was adapted to the creed of the Middle Ages. The name by which it was popularly known in Scotland, almost to the close of the last century, was that of the Purgatory Hammer. Found, as it frequently was, within the cist, and beside the mouldering bones of its old pagan possessor, the simple discoverer could devise no likelier use for it, than that it was laid there for its owner to bear with him 'up the trinal steps,' and with it thunder at the gates of purgatory, till the heavenly janitor appeared, that he might

" 'ask,
With humble heart, that he unbar the bolt.' "†

Beneath the cairns and barrows of the British Isles, and of the North of Europe, there is occasionally discovered a small spheroid ball of polished stone, resembling the stone cannou-

---

* Wilson's Archæology, p. 135.

† The arrow-head is known by the name of *Tordenkiler*, or Thunder-stone, by the Norwegian peasantry.

ball used in Scotland prior to the seventeenth century. It is difficult to conjecture the use to which these stones may have been applied by the early European races; but their association with the arrow-heads and celts of the same material, favours the opinion that they were employed as projectile weapons in the chase or battle-field. A highly-polished ball of red granite was found in a cist dug from a field on the estate of Cochno, Dumbartonshire; and another of flint was disentombed from a cairn on the moor of Glenquicken, Kirk-cudbrightshire.

An interesting specimen of the stone ball is noticed by Martin, in his account of Arran. It is described by him as a beautifully-polished jasper stone, "about the size of a goose egg," and was known in the Island by the name of "*Baul Muluy*"—the stone globe of Saint Molingus. The natives used it for the cure of diseases, and to swear the most solemn oaths by; and even during the present generation it has been consulted by the credulous Islanders. "Its virtue," says Martin, "is to remove stitches from the sides of sick persons, by laying it close to the place affected. If the patient does not outlive the distemper, it moves out of bed of its own accord."* It is also said to have been carried about by the M'Donalds of the Isles, and when engaged in battle, its possessors invariably secured the victory over their enemies. The name "*Baul Muluy*" has connected it with Saint Molingus of the Holy Isle, who is said to have been chaplain to the M'Donalds.† But tradition is at fault here; and Saint

---

* Martin's Western Islands, pp. 225, 226.   † Ibid, p. 226.

Muluy must have been the favourite Celtic Saint, Molocus, whose *Baculum More*—big staff—was carried before the Bishops of Argyll in their religious ceremonies.

The custody of the *"Baul Muluy"* was a hereditary privilege, which for generations was enjoyed by the Clan Chattan, or MacIntosh family, who were ancient followers of the M'Donalds. This curious relic was lost a few years ago by a gentleman to whom it was entrusted, who partook too much of the scepticism of the present age to appreciate its value.*

The belief in the healing efficacy of ancient stone missles appears to have been a common superstition in the Western Islands. The famous brooch of Lorn was adorned by a charm-fraught globe of crystal. The natives of Skye had their *Lapis Hecticus*, for the cure of diarrhœa; and in the Church of Saint Columba, in the little Flada Isle, there used to lie upon the altar a round blue stone, which was employed by the inhabitants in the cure of certain diseases, and prized by the fishermen as an unerring indicator of approaching storms.†

In these superstitions we may probably trace a remnant of the old magical system which so long prevailed in the East, and which is believed to have formed a prominent element of the Druidic theosophy of the British Isles. The *Chelonitides* was efficacious in appeasing storms; and the *Hematites, Erotylos, Cornu,* and *Ammonis,* like the *Lapis Hecticus* of Skye, and the *Baul Muluy* of Arran, were celebrated for

* Statistical Account.   † Martin's Western Islands.

their medicinal virtues.* Many of these gems and crystal
balls have been found in the Grecian and Roman sepulchres.†
The *perforated* pebbles of the British barrows, like the gems
of the East, may have been used by the early Britons as
charms or talismans. Such relics are still known in the
Scottish Highlands by the name of *Clach Bhuai*, or the
powerful stones, on account of the inherent virtues they are
believed to possess.

The monumental remains of the early inhabitants of Arran
are now fast disappearing from the Island, and soon all trace
of their existence shall have been swept away by the ravages
of time and the encroachments of agriculture. We would
fain catch a few gleams of light, whilst we may, from these
time-honoured records of the Arran of olden times, and of
the stirring scenes which were being enacted around its
shorelands and within its bosky dells, ere Time had began to
obliterate its landmarks and efface the footprints of its primeval colonists.

With feelings of instinctive reverence we gaze back through
the long vista of past ages, and recall the pulsings and throb-
bings of human life which lie entombed beneath the mossy
cairns and enlichened monoliths. Dark forests cover the face
of the Island, except where, here and there, the lofty summit
of some granite mountain rises bare and bleak. A few sub-
terranean huts, covered with heath and branches, cluster
around the shores and within the glens. Amidst the jungles
of Glen Cloy, Soordale, and Iorsa, the wolf, the brown bear,

* Humana gemmis attribuit Fata.—Pliny.
† Twenty spheroid gems were found in a single urn at Rome.

and the wild boar roam in search of prey.   With their
weapons of stone or flint, the rude Islanders pursue the deer
within its native woods; or, in their fire-hollowed canoes,
follow the whale as it gambols in Brodick Bay.*

The scene changes:—The sun has cast its setting rays over
a bloody battle-field; the Plain of Mauchrie is covered with
the dead and the dying, the heath is stained with their blood.
The victors gather their dead in silence; and within the
sacred covert the funeral pyre is lit, and the ashes of the
heroes are laid in their urns.   And so, "fancy unto fancy
linking," we wander amidst the old ruins of the primeval
past; and, whilst revelling in the beauty and sublimity of
Arran scenery, our impressions are hallowed and deepened
by the reminiscences and traditions of olden times which
float around us.

---

* In the carse lands of the Forth, harpoons of deer-horn have been
found beside the skeletons of whales, about twenty-five feet above the
full tide of the river.— *Wilson's Archæology*, *p.* 33.   See an interesting
account of the canoes of the Clyde in "Glasgow Past and Present,".
Vol. III., by John Buchanan, Esq.

PART II.

METALLURGIC PERIOD.

CHAPTER I.

Introduction.

DURING their wanderings amid the forest ranges of the European Continent, the early Allophylian and Celtic races appear to have lost all knowledge of the arts and civilisation of their birth-land. The relics disentombed from the grave mounds left in their track are the records of a people sunk in the lowest depths of barbarism and superstition.

For many centuries the rude primeval colonists of the British Isles followed the restless, nomade habits which their fathers had acquired in their westward wanderings. With their frail weapons of stone and flint, they fought for existence with the fierce denizens of the jungles and forests; and shadowed forth, in vast amorphous monuments, their vague convictions of an over-ruling and all-permeating Creative Power.

But, as time rolled on, another band of daring pioneers

K

emerged from the old cradle-land of the human race, carrying
with them the fruits of Eastern civilisation.   The ships of
Tyre and Carthage, freighted with merchandise, crowded the
Mediterranean.   A few adventurous galleys, bent on greater
enterprise, passed the Pillars of Hercules, sailed along the
coasts of Europe, and landed upon our shores.   The treasures
of the East were spread out before the astonished gaze of the
primitive Islanders, and the native wealth of Cornwall was
eagerly pledged to purchase them.

As intercourse and commerce increased, the stone hammer
and the lance-head of flint were flung aside for the spear and
the sword of bronze, and afterwards of iron.   Step by step
civilisation and population advanced, till the forest rang with
the stroke of the hatchet, fields were cleared and cultivated,
and houses and fortresses superseded the caves and subter-
ranean dwellings.

The earliest historic reference to the Cassiterides, or Tin
Mines of Cornwall, is made by Herodotus, who wrote about
the middle of the fifth century B.C., but it is probable "that
the Phœnicians traded with the miners of Cornwall and the
Scilly Islands at a much earlier period; if, indeed, we must
not look to these ancient Cassiterides as one of the chief
sources from whence even the Egyptians and Assyrians derived the tin with which they alloyed and hardened their
earliest tools."*

The nomade habits of the primitive Britons, and the spirit
of barterage introduced on the arrival of the Phœnician
traders, must have ere long diffused many of the products of

* Wilson's Archæology, pp. 194, 195.

Eastern civilisation over the whole of North Britain. The Caledonian forests supplied the hunter with the furs and the skins, which would be carefully preserved and exchanged for the coveted spear and sword of bronze.

Whilst the possession of these weapons must have long preceded the knowledge of their manufacture, the contents of the grave mounds which stud the straths of Caleydon and the shorelands of the Western Isles sufficiently attest the striking progress which the North Britons had made in the metallurgic arts prior to the Roman Invasion. Their spears, axes, and swords were ornate with the tasteful devices of the native designer; plates of silver and gold adorned their shields of bronze, and their spear-heads were chased with the beautiful fret-work of the sculptured monoliths. The bronze helmet which had covered the head of the warrior chief, the brooch which had clasped his sagum, the golden torc which had covered the shoulders and breast of the Druid priest, the silver ring which had enfolded the long, fair locks of the maid of Albion, and the jewelled coronet which had encircled her snowy brow, have been disentombed from their mossy beds, and now enrich and adorn our cabinets and museums.*

* Statistical Account, Archæologia, Gentlemen's Magazine, Wilson's Archæologia, etc.

CHAPTER II.

Forts and Camps.

"Nestling in the woody glen,
  Or perched on the tall summit
  Of the mountain cliff,
  The ruined walls are seen
  Of Camps and Fortlets—
  The primitive defence-works
  Of the early Britons."

As the possessions and pastoral wealth of the communities or
tribes of North Britain increased, an organised system of
defence was introduced for the protection of their territories
against neighbouring aggression. The little hamlet by the
shore, or within the copsewood of the glen, was entrenched
and fortified—camps were raised and envallumed in the dark
mountain hollows, and around the territorial landmarks, or
boundaries of the tribes, a series of forts was built of solid
masonry.

On the invasion of Calcydon by the Romans, many of
these primitive defences were scattered over the country.
Strabo and Diodorus Siculus describe Britain as "being for
the most part flat and woody, and having many strong
places on hills." These *places* were frequently besieged and
garrisoned by the Roman generals; and occasionally the

Castella of the invaders were raised in juxtaposition to the native strengths, to command and overawe them. The British forts on Eldon Hill, at Inch Stuthill, near the Tay, and on the height of Castle Over, appear to have been converted into Roman posts. The Roman camp, at Lyne Kirk, is placed within the cluster of British hill forts, which formed the defence of part of the Gadeni territories.*

After the lapse of two thousand years, the number of these native *strengths*, and the massive solidity of their construction, excite our surprise and admiration. In the neighbourhood of Blair Athol, within the circumference of a few miles, there are the ruins of no fewer than nineteen hill forts—the walls of which are, in many instances, nine feet in thickness. The White Caterthun, in Angus, is a remarkable specimen of the British fortress. It encloses an area of 430 by 200 feet, and is surrounded by a series of concentric ramparts and ditches. The ramparts are composed of an accumulation of large loose stones, forming a wall upwards of 100 feet thick at the base, and 26 feet thick at the top. "The vast labour," says General Roy, "which it must have cost to amass so incredible a quantity of stones, and carry them to such a height, surpasses all description." †

The number, position, and general arrangement of these and similar *strengths* throughout the Highlands and Isles, seem to indicate that they were erected by each tribe along the borders of its territories, as a defence against the aggres-

* Chalmers' Caledonia.
† Wilson's Archæology, pp. 412, 413.

sive inroads of its neighbours. When Agricola carried his conquests into North Britain, A.D. 81, the Hebrides, like the Mainland, were inhabited by certain communities or tribes, connected by a common origin, language and religion, but animated towards each other by feelings of jealousy and hostility, which frequently broke out into feuds and open warfare.

The Glottians, who inhabited Arran at the period of the Roman invasion,* were either a distinct tribe, or a branch of the Epidii† of Kintyre. In either case, their coasts were exposed to the raids of their more powerful and warlike neighbours, the Attacoti on the north, and the Damnii‡ on the east, who must have cast many an envious glance across the intervening sea, to the little Glotta Isle, with its rich pasture hills and its well-stocked hunting grounds.

To secure themselves against invasion, the Islanders looked well to the strength of their bows, and the keenness of their spears, girdled their coasts by a chain of forts, and built their camps within the secluded forest dell, or on the summit of the inaccessible mountain cliff. The Castles of Brodick, Loch-Ranza, Kildonan, and probably Lamlash, were the sole safeguards of the coasts of Arran during the fierce turbulency of the feudal ages, and the aggressive raids of the Reguli of

* Chalmers' Caledonia—see Map, also Maps of Ptolemy and Richard of Cirencester.
† Epidii—Ebyd—a peninsula.
‡ The Damnii were the most powerful and important of the Southern tribes of North Britain. They inhabited the straths of the Clyde, and the shires of Ayr, Renfrew, and Stirling.—*Ptolemy.*

Islay and Argyll; but centuries before these fortalices were erected, the estuaries, bays, and shorelands of the Island were protected by the fortresses and fortlets of the early Glottians.

In searching out these old strengths of Arran, we may start from the southern crescent of Lamlash Bay, in the direction of King's-cross. Clumps of stunted birch and hazel fringe the coast, but the beach is rough and rugged; the cliffs and shelves of red sandstone are intersected here and there by dark veins or dikes of trap, whilst huge crags and boulders of conglomerate and granite are tumbled about in wild confusion. Not a creek or inlet, or patch of sand or gravel, is met with where a canoe or galley could touch with safety, until we arrive at King's-cross. Here the coast is low and level, and a pebbly beach dips gently into the sea, where a few fishing wherries ride idly at anchor. On a little eminence, a few yards from the rocky ledge from which the patriot Bruce is said to have embarked for the Carrick shore, there are the remains of a circular fortlet, which appears to have commanded the landing-place and harbourage in early times. Its walls, now levelled with the rank grass, are about three feet in thickness, and enclose an area of fifteen feet in diameter. This is the smallest and most primitive of the Arran defences, and was no doubt built by its ancient inhabitants as a place of security, from which, with their spears and arrows, they might harass and oppose the landing of an invading enemy.

Rounding the Point, we follow the bold sweep of Whiting Bay, and reach Glen Ashdale, stretching inland from the shore between its green ridges. We wander along the mar-

gin of the meandering streamlet, through a forest of heath
and fern, startling the *caolacs dhu* or *rheadh* at every step,
and, passing the old chapel with its rude burying-place,
arrive at the falls of Eis-a-cranaig—a rich gem for the sketch-
book of the artist. Perched on the terrace of a precipitous
bank to the right are the remains of the primitive fortress of
Glen Ashdale. Its gray ruins are now overgrown with
feathery brushwood, but their extent and general appearance
sufficiently indicate the former massiveness and strength of
the building. Its walls are twenty-five feet in thickness,
formed of huge blocks of sandstone and granite, compactly
and solidly built, but without cement. The circumference of
the whole is about 280 feet.

From the situation of this strength, and the vast labour
which has been employed in rendering it impregnable to the
attacks of an enemy, it is probable that it was used as an
encampment by the early Islanders for the security of their
families in the event of invasion. In the neighbourhood,
there is the *Knocklecarleu*—Consultation Hill—where, as
tradition relates, the chiefs were wont to meet on the approach
of a hostile fleet, to devise means of defence. The frail huts
of the villagers have disappeared, but the Consultation Hill,
the Camp, and the old burying-place,* are the enduring
indications of an early population within the Glen and along
the shores of the Bay.

The next fort we meet in our ramble is that of Tor-Castle
—Castle Hill—a little to the north of Slaodridh, situated on
an artificial hillock, about fifty feet in height, near the shore.

---

* We refer to the large quantities of stone-chests found at Largiebeg.

It is a round building, 160 feet in circumference, with walls from four to five feet in thickness. An adjoining outpost, or defence of smaller extent, protects the narrow entrance from the sea. The principal strength is skilfully and massively constructed. Its walls are now demolished, but the foundation stones still remain—huge flat blocks of sandstone broken and chiselled by the native builder into regular and symmetrical proportions. On digging around the mound and within the ruins, we discovered large quantities of the bones of the ox, the boar, and the wild deer, mingled with the shells of the beach, and imbedded in a dark fetid loam.*

Similar traces of animal inhumation, and occasionally urns and *cistvæns*, have been disinterred from within the primitive forts of the Mainland. Human bones, deer horns, and lance-heads were found some years ago on removing the earth which filled the trenches of three British Duns, which crowned the ridge of rising ground above the valley of Dalrymple; and under the ruins of the walls of a native strength in the parish of Pittenain, Lanarkshire, there were found several stone-chests containing incinerated ashes.†

Like the Norse Sea Kings, who regarded the *Skibssætninger*, or the galley in which they fought and died, as the most honourable sepulchral monument to the bravery of their lives, the British warrior may have yearned for the distinction of a grave within the walls of the fortress in the defence of which he received his death-wound. It is said that a battle was

* Human bones are also said to have been found amongst the ruins.
† Chalmers' Caledonia, Vol. I., pp. 87–96. Wilson's Archæology, pp. 408–410.

fought long ago around the Tor-Castle, between the natives
of Arran and a band of marauders from Kintyre. The Arran
men were encouraged to victory by the cheers of their wives ⁓
and children, who crowded the Clappen Hill to witness the
conflict. After a desperate struggle the invaders were repulsed, and forced to seek safety in their ships.

Tor-Castle is further remarkable for the existence of ancient
plough-marks, popularly known as *elf-furrows*, which are
still clearly traceable over its summit. Tradition relates that
the rich black mould of the mound tempted the natives to
reduce it to cultivation. This was many years ago, when the
old *rig* system of farming obtained in the Island. The lands
of the neighbourhood were partitioned between twelve families,
each of which claimed a rig of the Castle Hill. The mound
was cleared of the rich verdure which mantled its surface,
and drills of cabbages were planted within the ruined walls.
But a signal retribution followed the commission of this
daring sacrilege. Before the year closed, the children of the
hamlet were fatherless, and eleven new graves were seen in
the little church-yard of the district. The villager who
escaped had been called to another part of the Island when
the old building was being turned into a household garden,
and thereby avoided the doom which befell his companions.
The people of Arran still regard the old fortlet with a
superstitious dread, and he is thought to have a bold heart
who will venture to disturb its ruins or visit them after
nightfall.

The popular tradition which prevails throughout the Lowlands respecting the origin of these early vestiges of hill cul-

tivation, relates "that at a time when Scotland was under a
Papal interdict, or sentence of cursing from the Pope, it was
found that his Holiness had forgot to curse the hills, though
he had commanded the land usually arable to yield no
increase, and that while this sentence remained, the people
were necessitated to seek tillage ground in places unusual
and improbable."*

Elf-furrows have been discovered on many of the heights
of Scotland, but they are of more frequent occurrence in that
portion of the Western Highlands occupied by the Dalriadic
colonists prior to the Scottish conquest, and have been supposed to indicate the existence of a very considerable population in those early times, possessing an intimate acquaintance
with the means necessary to, and the advantages arising
from, the agricultural development of their lands.† It is no
less probable, however, that at a period when the valleys and
straths of Caleydon were covered with dense forests and
marshy jungles, the heath-clad hills may have afforded the
readiest and most accessible tillage ground for the immediate
necessities of the newly-arrived colonists.

Leaving Tor-Castle, we continue our ramble along the
shore-road. The wavelets surge on the rocky beach beneath
us, and the brown hills on the right, flecked with granite
blocks, tower above in wild magnificence. Before us is the
bold promontory of Drumidoon, with its precipitous cliffs.
We pass the village of Blackwater-foot, with its little fishing
cots, and, threading our way between the shelving crags of

* Sinclair's Statistical Account, Vol. XVII., p. 115.
† Wilson's Archæology, p. 123.

the shore, ascend the ridge of the Doon, by a narrow path-
way trod out amid the tall heath.   In a few minutes we have
clambered over the ruined walls, and find ourselves within
the fortress.   Dark columnar cliffs, resting upon a base of
red sandstone, rise precipitously from the sea, to the height
of 300 feet.   From the northern *terminus* of the cliff, we
trace the ruins of the huge wall—eight to ten feet in thickness—which surrounds the broad flat summit of the hill
towards the land, and joins the extremity of the cliff on the
south, enclosing an area of several acres.   The remains of a
gateway may still be seen near the centre of the wall, which
appears to have been the sole entrance to the fortress.   Large
loose ledges of granite are strewn about within the interior
of the building, resembling the ruined *Weems*—uamha, a
cave—of Aberdeenshire.   This is unquestionably the most
interesting and important of the ancient strengths of Arran.
Its inaccessibility from the shore, and the elaboration of its
walled defences towards the land, must have rendered it a
place of impregnable security.   A great portion of the ruins
have been removed by the natives for the building of dikes,
houses, and other purposes; but even the imperfect remains
of this Cyclopean structure, and the incredible labour which
must have been employed in dragging such massive blocks
of granite up the steep acclivity of the hill, and rearing them
around its summit, excite our astonishment, and heighten
our estimate of the progress attained by the early Glottians
in many of the arts and appliances of civilised life.*

* These considerations led us at first to infer that the fortresses of
Drumidoon and Tor-Castle owed their origin to a later period than

Doon Fortress, Drumidom.

The numerous remains of sepulchral monuments scattered around, confirm the tradition that the Mauchrie Moor and the shores of the Blackwater were in ancient times the scene of a busy population; and it is probable that the elaborate fortifications of the Doon were used by the early Islanders as a place of retreat, on the invasion of an enemy, where their families, goods and cattle, might remain in safety, when their deserted cots by the shore, and the surrounding forests, were swept by the fire of the invaders.*

The natural position and architectural features of the Drumidoon, remind us of the fortified towns described by Cæsar in his Gallic campaign. When the Aduatuci were informed of the defeat of the Nervii, and of the approach of the Roman conquerors—"deserting all their towns and forts, they conveyed together all their possessions into one town eminently fortified by nature. While this town had on all sides around it very high rocks and precipices, there was left on one side a gently ascending approach of not more than 200 feet in width, which place they had fortified with a very lofty double wall; besides, they had placed stones of great weight and sharpened stakes upon the wall."†

Martin relates that the Drumidoon was used as a *girth* or

the forts on the eastern coast of the Island (Ed. *New Phil. Journal*, Vol. IX., Jan., 1859); but further investigation and *comparison* have convinced us that they are all the work of one period, and probably of the same people.

* The whole of the present population of Arran might be readily assembled within its walls.

† Cæsar's Comment. B. II., chap. xxix.

sanctuary, and "whatever number of men or cattle could get within it, were secured from the assaults of enemies—the place being privileged by universal consent." * Many of these consecrated places appear to have existed in Britain during the Roman invasion, and, like the *Ba-dhun*—Hill of Refuge—in Moray, were invested in later times by the *prestige* of antiquity and the halo of traditional consecration.

When the *girth* was abandoned, the chapel or cell of the Christians became the sanctuary for the criminal and the oppressed, and as early as the thirteenth century laws were enacted by the Scottish Kings for the regulation of these institutions:—" Gif any fleis to Halie Kirk, moved with repentance, confesses that he heavily sinned, and for the love of God is come to the house of God for safetie of himself, he sall nocht tine life nor limme, bot quhat he has taken frae anie man he sall restore sameikill to him." † But the early Glottians enshrined their *girth* with the sacredness of stone walls, and trusted their safety to the inaccessible security and impregnable defence-works of their retreat.

Before descending to our little snuggery at Blackwaterfoot, we are tempted to rest a while on a ruined *Weem*, and admire the rich and varied scenic panorama around and beneath us. The balmy ocean breeze fans our cheeks; the sea-fowl flaps his wings above us, and the hollow beat of the wavelets on the rocks beneath echoes in our ears. The setting sun has flung a roseate glow over the purple hills, and lit up the dark moorland of the Mauchrie with its chameleon beams. Nestling amid the trees, and bathed in the shadows

* Martin's Western Islands.   † Alexander II., c. 6.

of the hills beyond, are the white cots of Shiskin. The Clachan burnie and the Blackwater meander between emerald fields. North and south are the bays of Mauchrie and Drumidoon, with their fishing hamlets straggling along the golden sands of the shore, or embosomed in the copsewood which skirts the beach. The Atlantic waves roll between us and the dark headland of Kintyre—the stronghold of feudal chieftainship in olden times, and the tryst of many a lawless invasion of the Arran Isle and the Clutha shores.

Our next rest is at Loch-Ranza. We climb the green shoulder of Craig-na-Cuiroch, which rises from the southern shore of the Loch, and perceive the ruins of an old fort on a round *plateau* of the mountain ridge. It closely resembles, in extent and appearance, the strength of Tor-Castle, already described. By hurling down spears, missiles, and boulders from the walls of the Cuiroch-Craig, the ancient Islanders must have greatly harassed the landing of an invading foe, and cut off all access to the Glen by its principal entrance. The fort was visited by the present Emperor of the French in 1848.

From Loch-Ranza to Sannox, the shore is rugged and precipitous, but an excellent road has been cut over the hills, so we follow it and revel in the wild magnificence of mountain, brake, and mossy tarn around us. We join the shore at Mid-Sannox. On a rising ground to the right is a heap of gray ruins—the remains of the primitive defence which commanded the Bay in early times.

An hour's walk brings us to Brodick. The advance of agriculture around the shorelands of the Bay has obliterated many of the vestiges of ancient habitation noticed by Martin, Pennant, and MacCulloch. The barrows, cairns, and monoliths which studded the hills and glens a century ago, have been mostly demolished, and their ruins used for the construction of drains, dikes, and bridges; fulfilling the prophetic lament of the dying Conlach:—

> "Place that gray stone at my head,—
> But the son of future times will not know it;
> He will make it a bridge over some little stream
> Which he cannot bound across." *

The remains of the fort at Brodick were reserved for a nobler fate. On its site, and from its stones, the old castle of Bradewick is said to have been built;† but the castle has been so frequently razed and re-built, during the wars with England, that not a relic of the original building now exists.

Besides the fort, towering above the beach for the defence of the Bay, the prudent villagers had their encampment within the Glen, like that of Glen Ashdale, for the security of their wives and children, on the alarm of invasion. The entrance to Glen Cloy is by a dark narrow avenue, embowered by the richest foliage of the beech and fir. As we pass the mansion-house of the descendants of Fitz-Louis, the valley widens between its purple hills; but, following the stream, we shortly arrive at the camp. It is situated on a green artificial mound, about fifteen feet in height—known as the *Tornanshiain*—Faeries' Mound—nestling in the bosom of the glen, and buttressed on either side by the Faerie Hills,

---

* Smith's Translation of Cathula.
† Statistical Account.

the Black Hill, and the Craig-na-jolair—Eagles' Rock.
The walls of the building are from three to four feet in
thickness, enclosing an area of about ninety feet in circumference. This is the "stalward plas" situated in "ane
woody glen," in which Bruce and his followers resided before taking possession of Brodick Castle.*

> "The scenes are desert now and bare,
> Where flourished once a forest fair,
> When these waste glens with copse were lined,
> And peopled with the hart and hind."

The old fortress, too, is now in ruins; and the cave ex-
cavated by Douglas in the side of the mound as a place of
concealment—known as "Bruce's Cave"†—has been swept
away by the waters of the Cloy, which are here enlarged by
the runnels from the surrounding hills.

The fairies are believed to have been the latest tenants of
Tornanshiain. Their *elfin bolts* have been found scattered
over the moor of the glen; and within the ruined walls of
the camp there is a huge tabular block of granite

> "Where oft the faerie queen at twilight sat."‡

Leaving the "faerie haunted valley," the next fort we
reach is at Springbank, situated on a little knoll, a few feet
from the shore. It appears to have been but a small and
primitive *defence*—about fifteen feet in diameter, and circular
in formation. The rank grass has overgrown its demolished
walls; but around them may still be traced the remains of

---

* Statistical Account. Lord of the Isles, Canto V.
    † Local tradition.   ‡ Ibid.

M

an entrenchment of earth.   The fortlet at King's-cross, of the
same tiny dimensions, was probably used by the early inhabitants of the district as a mere covert, from which to
harass an enemy's landing, and thereafter abandoned for the
open field, or the fastnesses of the woods; but the vallum
encircling the *strength* at Springbank, proves that the Islanders were prepared to defend their position against all the
hazards of an invasion.

A few minutes' walk along the stony beach, and we arrive
at Dun-Fiun—Fion-gal's Fort—the connecting link of the
chain of Arran's fort defences.   A ridge of columnar trap
rises over a bed of red sandstone to a height of about 600
feet above the sea level.   Around the flat summit of the hill,
and following its configuration, are the ruins of a wall from
three to five feet in thickness—embracing an area of about
140 feet in circumference—the stones of which, says Mr
Headrick, bear the traces of vitrification.*   Towards the
south, the hill is ascended by a successive range of those
broad irregular terraces which invest many of the moat hills
and fortified sites of the Highlands.

But the most interesting and suggestive feature of Dun-
Fiun is its vitrified walls.   About the middle of the last
century the attention of the Antiquarian Society of London
was first directed to the discovery, that the walls of many of
the hill sites or forts of Scotland were burned or scorified,
and in some cases fused into a porous slag.   It was first conjectured that this remarkable phenomenon was the result of
volcanic agency, and that the hills whereupon vitrescency

* Headrick's Arran.

occurred, were simply the craters of extinct volcanoes. This theory was ably opposed by Mr John Williams,[*] who maintained that the vitrification was artificially induced as a cement for the consolidation of the loose stones of which the inner walls, and, occasionally, the outer defences of the forts are built. Then followed the hypothesis of Lord Woodhouse in 1787.[†] Grounding his opinion on the complete dilapidation and *partial* vitrescency of the walls, and presuming that wood had been used in elevating and strengthening them, his Lordship inferred that the fire of a besieging enemy may have swept over many of the primitive hill-forts, demolished their ramparts, and caused the scorification and fusion of their stones. A more recent and probable theory was that advanced by Sir George Stuart Mackenzie, who supposed that the vitrescency had been occasioned by beacon-fires lit upon the summit of the hill-sites, to signal the alarm on the approach of an invading foe.[‡]

History, sacred and profane, proves the antiquity and general prevalence of this mode of communication. It appears to have been known to the Jews in the days of Jeremiah, and employed even as early as B.C. 1406,—five centuries before the siege of Troy. From the Talmud, we learn that the appearance of the new moon at Jerusalem was announced to the captives at Babylon by hill-beacons:—

[*] Mr Williams was mineral surveyor and engineer for the forfeited estates of Scotland.

[†] Published in the Transactions of the Royal Society of Edinburgh.

[‡] This theory must have readily suggested itself to the mind of its originator, as the hill-beacon is the crest of the Mackenzies.

"Formerly fires were lighted on the tops of the mountains; but whether Samaritans led the nation into error (by lighting them at wrong places) it was ordained that messengers should be sent out. In what manner were these mountain fires lighted? They brought long staves of cedar wood, canes, and branches of the olive tree, also the coarse threads or refuse of flax, which were tied on the top of them with twine; with these, they went to the top of the mountains and lighted them, and kept waving them to and fro, upward and downward, till they could perceive the same repeated by another person on the next mountain, and thus on the third mountain, and so on."

The simplicity and effectiveness of the signal fire, as a means of communication, must have suggested its use and recommended its adoption to the warlike tribes of North Britain. The isolation, elevation, and relative positions of the British vitrified forts, admirably fit them for beacon sites. In some districts of Scotland these eminences may be seen commanding the straggling lines of common fortlets, which defended the inhabited districts, and girdled the territorial possessions of the tribes. Between the Moray Frith and Strath Tay, there are at least ten hill-forts, the walls of which are more or less vitrified.

The little Island of Bute had its thirteen forts, embraced between the signal sites of the Kyles on the north and Dun-a-goil on the south.* The Epidii of Kintyre had their coasts on the east and the west, guarded by the sites of Carradale and Dunskeig Hill,† and presuming that the Glottians were

---

* Statistical Account.   † Anderson's Highlands.

a branch of this tribe, the alarm of a hostile fleet menacing the southern or western shores of Arran may have been wafted across the Kilbrannan Sound by the friendly beacon in Carradale Bay.

The walls of Dun-Fiun consist chiefly of porphyry and sandstone, which would be fused by a very moderate degree of heat. The blazing fire of a few logs and branches, piled within the fort, would melt its walls into a vitreous mass, resembling opaque glass or porous slag.*

A better position for a beacon station than that of Dun-Fiun could not have been selected by the early inhabitants of Arran. It is situated towards the extreme east point of the Island, between the two important harbours of Brodick and Lamlash, and commands an uninterrupted view of the Clyde, as it opens into the Frith and expands into the Atlantic, whilst in the gray horizon the dark outline of the Ayrshire coast may be seen, which in these olden times was dotted and streaked by the strengths and hamlets of the warlike Damnii. A hostile fleet could not leave the opposite shores, or enter the Frith, without being observed by the wary sentinels of Dun-Fiun; and the signal fire would herald the alarm of invasion over the entire Island.

Such were the fortifications of Arran when the fleet of Agricola darkened the waters of the Clyde. They are but

---

* "The bonfire lighted on the summit of Arthur's Seat in 1842, to welcome the Queen on her first visit to Scotland, particularly fused numerous detached fragments of basalt, and imparted in some spots, to the depth of about half an inch, a vesicular structure to the solid rock beneath."—*Rambles of a Geologist, p. 366—Hugh Miller.*

rude monuments of primitive architecture, but the elaboration and massiveness of their construction must have rendered
them a formidable means of defence.

Their huge walls are now in ruins, "a gray mound of earth,
a moss-clad stone, lifting through it here and there its gray
head, are all that preserve their memory." But a romantic
interest hangs over these old remains, and could we but read
their history aright from the tangled web of mystic legend
and tradition which surrounds them, we might have many a
heart-stirring tale to tell of the heroic deeds of the brave
Glottians in defence of their Island home. The rocks and
the strata of the primeval world, buried far beneath the relics
of human life, have opened their stony archives to the
hammer of the geologist, and unfolded the history of our
Island, cycles of ages ago, when prowling mammalia were
the sole tenants of its virgin forests; and perchance, too, from
these later stone records, the fossil remains of human labour,
industry, and skill, we may catch some glimpse, however
faint, of the little Glotta Isle, when the hill forts rose entire
around its coasts, and the encampments nestled in the corries
of its glens:—

Clustering around its bays, and within its estuaries, are
the rude huts of the inhabitants. Fields of grain wave along
its alluvial shorelands, and herds of cattle graze over its
pasture hills. But now the galleys of the marauding Damnii
are being wafted by sail and oar across the dark bosom of
the Frith. Over the summit of Dun-Fiun, the signal fire is
lit, spreading the alarm from hill to hill. The women and
children are safely secured within the fastnesses of the woods

and the encampments of the glens. The shepherd leaves his flocks, the husbandman his fields—dingle and cliff re-echo the shrill war cry of the Glotta Isle. Higher still the beacon glows, till the sky is flushed with its ruddy glare, and the responding signal gleams brightly from the Carradale site. The galleys of the marauders are now nearing the Bay; but the forts of Brodick and Springbank are bristling with the spears and the arrows of the hardy Islanders, who crowd their walls, and line the beach, ready to repel a landing.

CHAPTER III.

Caves.

"Who was it scooped those stony waves?
Who scalped the brows of old Cairngorm,
And dug the ever-yawning caves?
'Twas I, the spirit of the storm.'"

WITHIN the level of the old sea margin, which has given to the coast scenery of Arran much of its pleasing picturesqueness and wild magnificence, the soft sandstone cliffs of the shore have been here and there riven into fissures by volcanic eruption, or honey-combed into caves by the ceaseless beat of the ocean waves.

These natural recesses were the primitive abodes of the primeval colonists of Arran, when the old forest ranges covered the Island; and even after its glens and bays were streaked with straggling hamlets, and its hills were crowned with fortlets, and the massive walls of its castles towered around its coasts, the sea-worn cave was the retreat, the hermitage, and the dwelling, of the exile, the recluse, and the hardy Islander.

Towards the base of Tor-an-righ—King's Hill—are the caves consecrated by the legendary residence of Fion-gal and Bruce. The King's Cave is a capacious water-worn recess, about 100 feet in length, 49 to 50 in width, and 55 in height, scooped out in a cliff of fine-grained sandstone. The *stratum* dips on either side, from a central vein which intersects the roof, forming a Gothic arch. Part of the same vein descends towards the back of the cave, in a perpendicular column, to the floor, leaving on each side a small narrow recess, now partially blocked up with stones from the shore. The whole bears a singular resemblance to the hull of a ship with its bottom upwards. Several rude representations of goats, sheep, and cattle, are carved over the southern wall of the cave. There are also dogs chasing stags, men shooting arrows, and similar devices, which are supposed to refer to the hunting exploits of Fion-gal and his heroes.

Fion-gal is said to have made Arran his resting-place when *en route* to the assistance of his allies in Ireland. He landed with his followers in a few rude birlings in the fine natural harbour of Mauchrie, and resided in the cave of Drumidoon. On his return from Ireland he spent a considerable time in Arran roaming through its forests with his favourite dogs. It was about this time that a son was born to him in the Doon cave. A straight groove is shown in the sandstone, of about two feet in length, which is believed to have been the exact size of the child's foot the day after his birth. From this infallible *datum*, the Rev. Mr Headrick has computed that Fion-gal must have been from seventy to eighty feet in height, and his wife from sixty to seventy!* The gigantic proportions of Ossian's hero are further attested by the tradition, that he formed a bridge of stepping-stones between his

* Headrick's Arran.

N

cave and the opposite coast for the convenience of himself
and his followers.

The legends of Bruce lend an additional charm to the cave
of Drumidoon. On the arrival of the exiled king from the
little Island of Rathlin, he is said to have resided for a time
in this rude retreat, sustaining the spirits of his friends by

> "Auld stories of men that wer
> Set in tyll hard assayis ser."

The streams and the woods provided for the frugal wants
of the little fugitive band; and there may still be seen the
holes for the support of the transverse beams that held the
pot in which the venison was seethed for the royal repast.
On the face of the column which descends from roof to floor,
there is the representation of a two-handed sword—the
claymore of the King—deeply, and not inelegantly, cut. *

Adjoining the King's cave, are his kitchen, cellars, larder,
and stable. The stable is much larger than the royal palace.
Its roof is supported by two massive pillars of red sandstone,
which give it the appearance of some old Gothic ruin.

At Kilpatrick, where the Hill of Learg-a-breac—Green
Furze Slope—meets the shore, is the Preaching Cave, a com-
modious water-worn recess.   It is still occasionally used,
being more central than the Parish Church. The song of
praise from this temple of Nature, mingling with the anthem
of winds and waves without, is in itself a deeply solemn
service, more impressive far than the organ's swelling notes,
or the chantings of white robed choristers.

* Local tradition; New Statistical Account; Headrick's Arran.

The Monster or Black Cave yawns beneath the bold cliffs of Benan Head, towards the south end of the Island. It is much the largest cave in Arran, and, like that at Kilpatrick, it has been used until lately as a place of worship by the Islanders. Within its walls the relics of ancient habitation have been discovered—arrow-heads, chipped and polished, and flakes of flint, mingled with the shells of the whelk and the limpet, indicating that here the native artist had his workshop and his kitchen, and wrought out from the rough pebble the frail weapons of the chase. Many of the rude implements of stone and flint which have been found in the moors and glens of the Island, may have been the work of the "ancient arrow-maker" of the Black Cave.

In the neighbourhood of the shooting lodge at Dippin, there is a dark recess which is believed to have a submarine communication with the Ayrshire coast. The old story of the piper and his dog was told us in connection with this cavern; and it is said that the muffled notes of the pibroch may still be heard at night rising and falling on the passing breeze.

There are several other caves and fissures around the coast of the Island; but though many of them are replete with scenic and geological interest, they are barren of historical or traditional attractions.

The Holy Island—the Melansay of the Norse writers—landlocks the broad Bay of Lamlash. It was here that Haco moored the remains of his shattered flotilla after his signal defeat at Largs. Its geological features are similar to those of the greater part of Arran. Huge masses of claystone and

porphyry have pierced through the normal *strata* of sandstone, and now tower above it in precipitous columnar cliffs
to the height of a thousand feet.   The barren ruggedness of
the islet is pleasingly relieved by clumps of brushwood, tufts
of blooming heath, and the emerald leaves and crimson
berries of the *Arbutus.*

The cave of Saint Molios, on the west coast, is a small
water-worn recess, about twenty-five feet above the present
sea-level, scooped out in the sandstone.   A shelf cut in the
side of the cave is pointed out as the bed of the Saint.   His
bath is within the tide mark of the shore below.   A few yards
to the south is the Saint's Chair—a square block of red
sandstone, surrounded by steps or seats; and near it is his
spring of pure water, which was long resorted to by the
people of Arran on account of its healing virtues.

The caves of Scotland were the primitive cells of the early
Culdee missionaries.   Saint Columba and Saint Cormac had
their caves on the Argyllshire coast; and Saint Mungo had
his bed, his bath, and his chair near the Molendinar Burn.
There is a cave in Knapdale containing an altar, a font, and
a cross cut in the solid rock.*

The cave of Saint Molios was the shrine of many a weary
pilgrimage a few centuries ago.   Itinerant devotees from the
Scottish Mainland and the outer Hebrides, and pious monks
in long white robes from the adjoining monastery, flocked to
the saintly hermitage, to count their beads and offer their
orisons.   The initials and monograms of these pilgrim visitors
may still be seen scratched over the roof of the cave; and

* Chalmers' Caledonia, Vol. I.   New Statistical Account.

there is a Runic inscription, neatly and regularly cut in characters of about an inch and a half in length, of which the following is a representation:—

The latter inscription Dr Wilson has translated thus:— *Nikulos ahane raist*—Nicholas engraved, or cut, this cave. The initial cross is the symbol of an ecclesiastic. It appears from the Chronicon Manniæ, that on the death of Bishop Michael in 1193, he was succeeded by a native of Argyll, called Nicholas. The coincidence of name and place of nativity is remarkable, and renders the supposition extremely probable that the pilgrim Rune engraver of the cave, was none other than Nicholas, the Bishop of Man.*

The cliff adjoining the hermitage has been long remarkable for its carbuncle, but like the gem of the Ward Hill referred to by Sir Walter Scott, "though it gleam ruddy as a furnace to those that view it from beneath, it ever becomes invisible to him whose daring foot scales the precipices whence it darts its splendour."

* Wilson's Archæology, pp. 531, 532.

CHAPTER IV.

Miscellaneous Relics.

MANY valuable relics of the precious metals have been found in Arran, which might have proved of great importance in illustrating the pre-historic annals of the Island, but the late impolitic law of treasure-trove, by which all such articles became the property of the Crown, has invariably led to their concealment and destruction.

The following account of a few of the metallic remains discovered in Arran is given either from particulars gleaned from the finders themselves, or from the *corroborative* evidence of persons by whom they were examined.

On the farm of Catacol, there was dug up, some years ago, from beneath a large stone, an urn or jar of unbaked clay, containing silver coins and a gold chain of the common linked pattern. The treasure was sold for a few pounds to a goldsmith in Ardrossan. Jars containing coins are also said to have been found in the caves of the Holy Island. A quantity of silver coins was discovered in one of the graves of the old burying-place in Glenashdale.*

* New Statistical Account.

In a cist, which a labourer turned up several years ago in making a fence round his garden, "there was found a piece of gold in the form of a handle of a drawer, with some iron or steel much corroded at each end. The man concealed his prize till he got it disposed of to a jeweller in Glasgow, who melted it down into rings and brooches."[*] Dr Wilson has identified this relic with the *ringa eldingham*, or bright rings, so frequently mentioned by the Scandinavian scalds, and which appear to have been used either as a circulating medium, or as ornaments for the person in early times.[†]

Sturla, in his "Raven's Ode," describes the men of Bute as "the forlorn wearers of rings," and the Norse invaders as "the steel-clad exactors of rings." Rings, bracelets, and armillæ of gold and bronze have, however, been frequently disentombed from the ancient British grave mounds—the relics of a period long prior to Norwegian or Roman invasion.

An interesting specimen of the copper cauldron was found a few years ago, on the farm of Auchincairn. It measured about sixteen inches in diameter, by twelve inches deep, formed entirely of one piece, and supplied with ring handles, which were fastened by small bolts or rivets. Three vessels of the same metal, and similar pattern, are said to have been dug up from the moss in Glen Cloy.

Kettles and cauldrons of bronze and copper have been found in Scotland, Ireland, and the north of Europe. Cauldrons were conferred as prizes at the public games of Greece

---

[*] New Statistical Account.   [†] Wilson's Archæology, p. 322.

and Rome,* and they appear represented as part of the spoil
and tribute of the Assyrians in the sepultures of Nimrod and
Kouyunjik.†

A mysterious importance was attached to these vessels in
ancient times, apart from their supposed use as utensils for
culinary purposes, and even in comparatively recent times
they were greatly prized by their fortunate owners, less, probably, on account of their intrinsic value than of the inherent
virtues they were imagined to possess:—

> "I received my genius
> From the cauldron of Ceridwen,"

says the poet Taliesin.   Among the articles of value bequeathed
by Cahir Mor, King of Leinster, to his family, were fifty copper
cauldrons.   And the biographer of St Patrick informs us that
whilst the Saint was at one time wandering through a forest
in Dumbartonshire, he was taken captive by a band of
marauders, and bartered for a kettle!

An iron sword, much oxidized, about three-and-a-half feet
in length, was found beneath the peat in Monie-mhor Glen.

An anchor of curious shape and workmanship; of a size

---

* "All the people, by Achilles still
Detained, there sitting, form'd a spacious ring,
And he the destin'd prizes from his fleet
Produc'd, capacious *cauldrons*, tripods bright,

.   .   .   .

Fair prizes to the swiftest charioteers."
—*Homer's Iliad.*

† Monuments of Nineveh, first series, plate 24; and second series,
plate 35.

capable of securing a vessel of fifty to sixty tons, was found several years ago a little to the north of the Whitehouse, in Lamlash—a few yards from the site of the old castle.* This discovery seems to confirm the tradition that long ago, ere the castle was demolished by the ravages of Time or the attacks of an invading foe, the galleys which entered the Bay for safety were anchored beneath its walls.

An anchor of similar form to the above was found on the hill-side in Glen Cloy, a full mile from the present tide-mark, and a little above the old sea margin. It was immediately taken by the finder to the smithy at Invercloy, where it was wrought down into shoe-nails for the Arran fillies.

The incessant abrasion of the granite—*la maladie du granite*—and the washing down of the loosened particles by the runnels of the hills must have effected considerable changes in the coast scenery of Arran since the time when the fleet of Agricola crowded the Clyde. The encroachments of the land upon the sea are strikingly exhibited in the sand banks and deltas of the principal bays and estuaries of the Island; and there can be little doubt that a few centuries ago the ships of the Islanders found a secure harbourage within the creeks or bays where the heath and brushwood now luxuriate.

The circumstance, that the anchor of Glen Rosa was found a few yards above the old sea margin, does not militate against the supposition that the Glen was at one time an inlet of the Broad-creek—Brodick. We cannot conceive for what purpose this heirloom of the sea could have been carried such a distance from the present tide-level; but we can readily

* See Chapter on "Castles."

imagine that it may have been hastily thrown on the rising bank of the Rosa creek, and left there by the improvident sailors of an Island galley.

Anchors, cables, and oars have been dug up from the Lochar Moss, Dumfriesshire, about twelve miles from the present flood-mark;* and the rude canoes of the adventurous Cluthians have been found beneath the busy streets of St Mungo.

In a field to the south of the Whitehouse there may be seen the vestiges of an iron forge. On removing a heap of dross and vitrified stones, we found the gravelly soil beneath, fused into a solid, slag-like mass. A weight and ball of iron were picked up beside the long-extinguished ashes of this primitive workshop.

* Wilson's Archæology, p. 31.

PART III.

CHRISTIAN PERIOD.

CHAPTER I.

Historical Introduction.

A MORE discriminative examination into the testimony of Greek and Roman writers, combined with the more trustworthy evidence of archæological investigation, has at last succeeded in dispelling much of the obscurity and obloquy which have long hung over the history of the early Britons.

From beneath the cairn, the barrow, and the monolith, antiquarian research has disinterred the records of a civilisation, the existence of which has been jealously ignored or grudgingly admitted by modern historians, though the discoveries of archæology have been amply confirmed and illustrated by the few incidental references of classic writers.*

The indomitable bravery, the ardent love of freedom, and the superior military appliances of the British tribes, elicited the admiration of Rome's ablest generals. Tacitus admits

---

* See Antoninus and Strabo.

that Cæsar by his two campaigns made only the discovery
of Britain, and not the conquest of it. The victories of
Claudius, Suetonius Pauliuus, and Ostorius Scapula, were
fiercely contended. Seventy thousand Roman citizens and
allies are said to have perished in the destruction of Cama-
lodunum and Verulam,* and fifty thousand Roman troops
fell in the attempt of Severus to punish the incursions of
the Caledonians.†

When Rome was in its infancy, a commercial intercourse
was established between Cornwall and the markets of the
Mediterranean; and when Cæsar first landed in Britain, its
population was so great as to excite his astonishment:—
hominum infinita multitudo est.‡ Its colleges were crowded
with students, and frequented by the *élite* of Gaul. " The
Druids," says Cæsar, "discuss and impart to the youth many
things with respect to the extent of the world and of our
earth, and respecting the nature of things."§ The system
of their religion resembled in many of its dogmas the theosophy introduced by Pythagoras; and was incomparably
superior in its purity and tendency to the dominant pantheistic mythologies of Greece and Rome.

The same Celtic people who opposed the landing of Cæsar
in the south met the aggression of Severus in the north, and
from their hill-forts watched the galleys of Agricola, as they
sailed along the shores of the Western Islands.

Though the fleet of Agricola may have anchored within

* Tacit. Vita Agricola. Xiphilinus says "eighty thousand."
† Giles' Ancient Britons, Vol. I., p. 238.
‡ Cæs. de Bello Gal., IV.   § Cæs. Comment. B. VI., c. xiv.

the bays and the creeks of the Hebrides, these Islands appear to have been but imperfectly known, even in number or geographical position, to the classic historians. Pliny, the first who mentions the " Hæbudes," enumerates them at thirty,* whilst Solinus and Ptolemy agree in reducing the number to five—Skie, Lewis, Rathry, Mull, and Ilay.† It is probable that there would be more to repel than to invite the curiosity and cupidity of the Roman circumnavigators in the wild, mountainous appearance of these surf-beaten Islands, surrounded by tides, currents, rocks, and skerries.

The Island of Arran—the *Glotta Insula* of Antonine's commentators—is passed over in utter silence by the classic itinerants, notwithstanding the Roman fleet must have frequently darkened its shores when making for the harbourage of Alcluyd.‡ The progress of the Roman legionaries has been accurately traced by means of the roads, walls, camps, and weapons which they have left behind them; but no such evidence has yet been discovered to indicate that they had ever landed on the Glotta Isle.

Within a century after the withdrawal of the Roman armies from Britain, A.D. 503, the Scoti-Irish—a cognate Celtic race—succeeded in effecting a settlement within the mountainous passes of Argyllshire, under Loarn, Fergus, and Angus, the three sons of Erc.§ A friendly intercourse and

---

* Pliny, lib. iv., c. xvi.   † Ptolemy, p. 34.
‡ Alcluyd, or Dumbarton.
§ Innes' Crit. Essay, Vol. II., pp. 689–694. There is a hill in Arran called *Suidhe-Fheargus*, upon which the son of Erc is said to have sat, and surveyed his kingdom.

alliance appear to have existed between the Picti of North Britain, and the Scoti of Ireland, during the occupancy of Britain by the Romans. Sidonius Apollinaris mentions the Scots among the enemies of Cæsar; and, about A.D. 360, large numbers arrived in the Glottæ Æstuarium—Frith of Clyde—and swept with fire and sword the coasts of the Romana Provincia.

The Dalriadic* colonists gradually strengthened their position by intermarriage with the Picts; and, by fostering the mutual jealousies and civil dissensions between the Cruithne, or Picts of the North, and the Piccardach, or Southern Picts, succeeded in extending their territories in the west, until, in 843, they placed their leader, Kenneth M'Alpin, on the throne of Scotland.†

Though rude, primitive, and warlike, the Scoti-Irish, who had thus established their ascendancy, and given their name to Scotland, were not ignorant of, or indifferent to, the arts of civilisation. From the middle of the fifth, till near the close of the eighth century, the Pictish and Saxon youth passed over to Ireland for their education, and, from the monasteries of Ulster, Christianity spread its conquests over the Western Islands and the Scottish Mainland, crushing out the old Druidic barbarities, and softening down the wild turbulencies of civil contentions.

To the Dalriadic period Mr Wilson assigns the origin of those remarkable plough-marks, or *elf-furrows*, which appear

---

* Dal-Riada—Portion of Riada. A district in the north east of Ireland.

† Chalmers' Caledonia, Vol. I., p. 304.

on many of the heath-clad hills of the Western Highlands, "startling the believer in the unmitigated barbarism of Scotland, prior to the medieval era, with evidence of a state of prosperity and civilisation."* Tradition, too, dwells fondly over this early period, flooding the Highland glens with the romance of Fion-gal and his heroes. The harp of Ossian has left its dying echoes amongst the village cots of the Arran Isle.†

It is probable that the success of the Dalriadic Revolution was mainly due to the assistance of the Cruithne or Northern Picts; and the conditions of this alliance were soon explained in the occupation by the Cruithne—under their leader Oree or Aurn—of Argyll, the Isle of Man, and the Southern Isles, (including the Island of Arran,) and which, along with Lochaber and Wester Ross, thereafter received the designation of Oirir Gael,‡ or the Coastlands of the Gael, in contradistinction to their inland territories.§

Aurn had scarcely taken possession of his peacefully-acquired conquests, when his security was rudely disturbed by the arrival of a foreign foe, the daring Vikings of the North:—

> "O'er the sun's mirror green
> Came the Norse coursers,
> Trampling its glassy breadth
> Into bright fragments.
> Hollow-back'd, huge bosom'd;

* Wilson's Archæology, p. 123.
† Ossian is said to have died in Arran. Statistical Account.
‡ Oirir Gael—hence Argyll.
§ Skene's Highlanders of Scotland, Vol. II., p. 29.

Fraught with mail'd riders,
Clanging with hauberks,
Shield, spear, and battle-axe;
Canvas-winged; cable-rein'd
Steeds of the ocean."

Cradled amidst the waves which lash the rock-bound shores
of Norway, and inspired with a fierce, fearless love of danger,
these Norse Vikings issued from the fiords and bays of Scandinavia in their raven-pennon'd galleys—the terror of every
northern sea and neighbouring coast.

Incited by love of enterprise and discovery—tempted, too,
by the wealth of foreign climes, these hardy navigators,
guided by the stars alone, steered their ships into un-
known seas, landed upon the shores of Greenland, Iceland,
and the Faroe Islands, and gazed upon the sunny forest-lands
of America, more than three centuries before Columbus set
sail for the West.*

A commercial intercourse appears to have been established
between the Scandinavians and the inhabitants of the Western
Islands prior to the Dalriadic invasion;† but peaceful pursuits were repugnant to the wild, restless spirits of the
Norsemen, and obnoxious to their heathen deities. The
favours of Odin and Thor were granted alone to the brave of
heart and the daring in deeds; and the goddess Hilda, with
her weird sisters, hovered over the field of slaughter to convey
the dying heroes to the halls of Walhalla. And so the Norse
rovers went forth in their dragon-prowed galleys to grapple

* Worsaee's Danes and Norwegians.   † Ibid.

with the Storm-King; and seek new conquests in distant battle-fields.

The terrible Dubhgall chief — Regner Lodbrog — after devastating the coasts of England, made an attack upon the Sudreyjar, A.D. 855.* Aurn, the King of the Oirir Gael, was slain in the conflict, and the men of the Isles were forced into the service of the Dubhgall chief, and compelled to join him in his piratical aggressions.†

The wild, lawless life of the Viking had much in it congenial to the bold, free spirit of the Gael. The same restless love of excitement animated the breast of each, and the Gall-gael soon followed the roving life of the Norsemen for very love of it. Side by side their galleys ploughed the British seas; side by side they fought, and together they shared the spoils of their plundering excursions; and not more dreaded along the coasts of the Scot or the Saxon were the daring Vikings of the North, than the roving, loving Skotar-Vikings of Arran and Argyll.‡

Under their leader, Regner Lodbrog, the Norsemen and the Gallgael invaded the Norwegian territories in Ireland, A.D. 856, and subsequently harried the Western coasts of England. During one of these expeditions, Regner was

---

* The Western Islands were divided into the Sudreyjar and the Nordreyjar by the Norse writers. The former comprised all the Islands to the south of Mull; the latter, Mull, and all the Islands north of it.

† Chron. No. III. in Innes' App.

‡ The Gaels of the Western Isles early received the name of Skotar-Vikings or Gallgael—Gaelic pirates. Arefroida, the oldest Norse writer we are acquainted with, mentions the occupation of the Hebrides by the Skotar-Vikings.

driven by a storm on the shores of Northumberland. Ella, the Anglo-Saxon King, hastened to attack his scattered forces, which he met and defeated, taking their chief, with many of his followers, prisoners.   On refusing, with Norse pride, to make known his name,* the brave Regner was thrown into a pen filled with snakes, and there died with the *swan's-song* on his lips—"*Grynte vilde Grisene Kjendte de Galtens Skjebne*"—how the young pigs would grunt if they knew the old boar's fate.†

Aulaf and Ivar, the sons of the Viking chief, on hearing of their father's fate, raised a large force to avenge his death, and being joined by Caittil-fin, who had succeeded Aurn as leader of the Gallgael under Regner, invaded and devastated the coast of Northumberland.   Ella, the King, was taken prisoner, a blood eagle was carved upon his back by the sons of Regner, and he was left to die in the forest pen, where their father had sung his last *swan's-song.*‡

Following up their success, Aulaf and Ivar sailed up the Clyde, harried its shores, and after a siege of four months, took possession of the fortress of Alcluyd.§

Meantime Harald Harfager—the fair-haired—had succeeded in conquering and consolidating the three-fold kingdom of Norway, Sweden, and Denmark into one monarchy,

---

* "I have been renowned in battle, but I never told my name to foe; yield to me, then shalt thou know that the mark of my sword is in many a field."—*Ossian's Poems.*

† Worsaee's Danes and Norwegians, p. 33.   ‡ Ibid, p. 33.

§ Annals of Ulster.   Ware's Antiq. Hibern, p. 108.

and in establishing himself king, A.D. 888.* The hostile chiefs, who had resisted his usurped supremacy, betook themselves to their ships, and escaped to the Western Isles; thence issuing in great numbers, they invaded the fiords, and pillaged the coasts of the new kingdom of Norway, and returned loaded with booty to their sea-girt retreats.

Harald, provoked by these outrages, assembled a large fleet, swept the western seas of the ships of these rebel chiefs, subdued the Islands which had afforded them shelter, and after establishing Sigurd—one of his followers—Jarl of Orkney and Shetland, and leaving a few of his bravest Vikings in the Western Isles to secure his conquests, he returned to Norway with much booty and many fair captives.†

No sooner, however, had the galleys of Harald left their shores, than the native chiefs of the Hebrides rose against their foreign oppressors, slew many of them, and expelled others from the Islands.

On the news of this revolt reaching Norway, Harald created Ketil—the son of Biorn—a chief of high rank, Jarl of the Hebrides, and despatched him with a powerful fleet, to reconquer the Isles, and hold them in tributive dependency to the kingdom of Norway. The success of Ketil's mission was complete, but no sooner had he subdued the Gallgael chiefs than he proceeded to establish the independence of his Jarldom, by strengthening his fleet, forming alliances with the rebel Vikings who still infested the western seas of Europe, and finally by proclaiming himself King of the

---

* Torfæus' History of Norway, Vol. II., b. ii., c. xii.

† Torfæus' Orcades, pp. 10, 11.

Hebrides.* He was not long fated, however, to enjoy his treacherously-acquired honours. He died soon after, and was consecrated to Odin, with the spear mark on his breast.

Ketil was succeeded by Niel, a native Gallgael chief, A.D. 914, who was slain by his brother Sidroc.† On the success of the Northumberland expedition, Sidroc, who had married the daughter of Ivar Beenlöse—the boneless—was put into possession of the territories of Ella, and, on the murder of his brother, became independent King of the Isles and Northumberland.

Freed from the galling yoke of their Norwegian conquerors, the Skotar-Vikings assumed their old restless predatory habits. Secure within their Island and Highland fastnesses, they made frequent raids into the straths and glens of Scotland; whilst the galleys of Arran, Kintyre, and Islay invaded the Frith of Clyde, and harried the coastlands of the Saxon Lowlanders. An unrelenting hostility to the Scotch and Saxon intruders long continued to burn fiercely in the breasts of the descendants of Aurn; and for several centuries the lawless Islemen were known as the Viking or pirate Scots. The cairn-covered moors of Arran, Argyll, and the outer Hebrides are the traditionary battle-fields of many a fierce feud and raid of clan and race.

But a common danger now menaced the independence of Scotland and the Western Isles, and induced a temporary alliance between the Scot and the Viking-Gael. From Ire-

---

* Torfæus' History of Norway, Vol. II., c. xxix.

† Niel and Sidroc are supposed to have been the issue of a Norwegian and Gaelic marriage.—Skene.

land, hordes of Norse pirates invaded the islet coasts of Scotland on the west, and from the south the Anglo-Saxons pressed northwards, spreading themselves over the Lowlands, and threatening to inundate the whole of North Britain. Aulaf, the son and successor of Sidroc, who is styled *"Rex plurimarum insularum"* by Saxon chroniclers, in order to secure a powerful ally in protecting his territories from foreign aggression, married the daughter of the Scottish King, Constantine III. The kingdom of Northumberland, won from Ella by the sons of Regner Lodbrog, was invaded and wrested from the Gallgael by Athelstane, the Anglo-Saxon king. Aulaf fled to Ireland, and returned with 600 ships and a large force of northmen, joined the Sudreyjar and Scottish fleet under Constantine III., off the Island of Arran, landed on the shores of the Humber, and met the army of Athelstane near Brunanborg, A.D. 937.* The Norse Sagas tell of the valour and daring of Aulaf and his brave auxiliaries in the celebrated battle of Brunanborg; but the numbers and determined resistance of the Saxons prevailed, and the broken forces of the Viking king were driven to their ships in hasty retreat. †

Aulaf was succeeded by his nephew, Maccus MacArailt; but the ascendancy of the Saxons was now complete. They not only retained possession of Northumberland, but reduced to tributive subjection many of the Islands of the Gallgael.

To Maccus, succeeded his brother, Gofra MacArailt, as

---

* Worsaee's Danes and Norwegians, p. 34.
† Annals of Ulster. Ware's Antiq., c. xxiv.

King of the Isles, who was slain in an Irish expedition, A.D. 989.

The Islesmen, weakened by their struggles with the Saxons, now became a prey to the ambition of Sigurd II., Earl of Orkney. On the death of Gofra, Sigurd collected a large fleet from the Orkney and Shetland Islands, conquered the Hebrides, deposed their native chief, and appointed Gilli, a Norwegian of high rank, Jarl of the Isles.

The Scottish King, Malcolm II., took advantage of Sigurd's absence to invade, by sea and land, his possessions in the North of Scotland; and no sooner had the Earl returned to the Orkneys, than Ragnal, the son of Gofra MacArailt, instigated and assisted by the deposed native chiefs, wrested the Isles from Gilli, and established himself King of the Hebrides.

Sigurd, roused by these outrages, determined to punish the rebels and aggressors. After reducing and plundering the Western Islands, he invaded the Scottish territories with a large force, met and defeated the army of Malcolm on the banks of the Beauley, and carried his devastations as far as the Frith of Tay.

> "The dwellings were all destroyed,
>   When he burnt every where;
>   Danger and death were not awanting,
>   As among dry reeds, the red flames
>   Sprung into the kingdom
>   Of the Scots." *

Meantime the Norwegian power in Ireland was threatened

* Torfæus' Orcades.

by the Irish, under Brian, their King. Sigurd collected a large fleet from the Orkneys and Western Islands, and hastened to the assistance of his kinsman—Sigtryg, King of Dublin. Bravely the Norsemen fought on the bloody field of Clontarf, but victory was against them. The forces of Sigurd were scattered and driven to their ships, and their brave chief was left amongst the slain, with the raven-pennon, which his mother wove, wrapped around him as a winding-sheet.*

For about twenty years after Sigurd's death, the Gallgael appear to have governed the Isles by their own native chiefs.

In 1034 they were reconquered by Earl Thorfin, the son of Sigurd II. Thorfin possessed all the ambition and fierce daring of his father. He pushed his conquests into the very heart of Scotland, wrested nine Jarldoms from the Scottish King, and compelled the Ostmen of Ireland to pay him tribute. But as age crept over the brave Earl, he grew weary of raid and conquest. From a Culdee recluse, he had gathered some stray truths of the Christian faith, and with a new fervour stirring his soul, he set out on a pilgrimage to Rome, where he received the "indulgence" and blessing of the Pope. On his return to the Orkneys, he replaced the raven-pennon which had waved over many a victorious battle-field, with the banner of the cross encouraged the progress of Christianity throughout his dominions, and reigned peacefully till his death in 1074.†

When the news of Thorfin's death reached Ireland, the Ostmen shook off their allegiance, and in the flush of their

* Ware's Antiq., pp. 114, 115.   † Orkneyinga Saga, p. 87.

restored independence, swept the coasts of Scotland with fire
and sword; whilst Diarmed, the son of Maclnambo, King of
Dublin, invaded the territories of the Gallgael, and established
himself King of the Isles.

He was succeeded by Godred—son of Sitric, an Irish chief
—upon whose death Fingal MacGodred became "*rex Insularum.*"

On the defeat of the Norwegians by Harold, King of England, at the battle of Stainford Bridge, Godred Crovan—the
white-handed—who led the army of the King of Norway, fled
to the Hebrides with a few galleys, and deposed Fingal, the
Gallgael King, and expelled him from the Isles.   After reducing the native chiefs to subjection, Godred sailed for the
Irish coast with a large force of Skotar-Vikings, and eventually
succeeded in conquering Dublin and a great part of Leinster.*

Meantime, the growing power of Godred excited the
jealousy of the Norwegian King, Magnus Barefoot.   Overtures
of alliance were made by Magnus to Malcolm Canmore, King
of Scotland, and a treaty entered into, importing the con-
cession to Norway of all the Islands on the west coast of
Scotland which could be circumnavigated by a sailing ship.
After subjugating the Isles, Magnus caused his ship to be
dragged over the narrow isthmus which connects the peninsula
of Kintyre† with the Mainland.   The crafty king sat himself
at the helm, and steered his galley through the channel cut
out in the forest glade by the hauberks and axes of his
followers; and, by this wily artifice, Kintyre was wrested from

---

* Gregory's Highlands and Isles, p. 6.
† Now Tarbert—a place over which vessels can be dragged.

Scotland, and united with the Sudreyjar or South Isles, in tribute to the kingdom of Norway, A.D. 1093.*

Magnus having deposed Godred, and established his son Sigurd, King of the Isles, returned to Norway with his fleet, where he introduced the Highland dress amongst his subjects. Snorre Sturleson, the Icelandic historian, who wrote towards the beginning of the thirteenth century, says:—"They," the King and his followers, "went about the streets with bare-legs, and wore short coats and cloaks, whence Magnus was called by his men 'Barford' or 'Barbeen,' 'Barefoot' or 'Barelegs.'" †

On the death of Magnus, Sigurd, his son, was crowned King of Norway. Godred Crovan died in Islay shortly after his defeat, leaving three sons, Lagman, Harald, and Olave. Lagman, the eldest, succeeded to the throne of the Isles, vacated by Sigurd; but, after an unchequered reign of seven years, he departed on a pilgrimage to the Holy Land, where he died.‡

Donald M'Fade, an Irish prince, was chosen regent during the minority of Olave,§ and soon after was expelled from the Isles by his rebellious subjects. Olave the Red, sur-named the "Bitling" by Norse writers, now became King of

---

* Magnus Barefoot's Saga. As late as the seventeenth century the peninsula of Kintyre was classed among the South Isles by the Scottish Parliament.

† Worsaee's Danes and Norwegians, pp. 288, 289.

‡ Chron. Manniæ.

§ Harald appears to have died during the reign of his brother Lagman.

Q

the Sudreyjar. He is designated, in Saxon chronicles, "*Rex Manniæ et Insularum.*"*

Since their subjugation by Regner Lodbrog, the native Gallgaels had never ceased their struggles to throw off their allegiance to the crown of Norway; but the preponderance of the Norsemen in the Western Islands rendered every attempt to regain their independence ineffectual. Throughout Kintyre, and the immediately contiguous mainland, however, their numerical strength was less formidable, and the native chiefs were frequently successful in expelling their Viking oppressors from their territories, and driving them into their Island fastnesses.

During one of the pillaging raids of the Norwegians under Olave the Red, the great Somerled is first introduced to Scottish history. His father, Gillibrede—a petty Skotar Gaelic chief—of Morven, was dispossessed of his lands, and forced to seek refuge amongst the forests of his native glens, from the Saxon supporters of Edgar, son of Malcolm Canmore, whose claim to the crown of Scotland he had determinedly opposed.

Gillibrede is known to tradition as *Gillibrede na'n Uaimh,* or Gill of the Cave, and the mountain recess amidst the Morven wilds, where the old chief lay concealed from his Anglo-Saxon foes, is still regarded with feelings of reverence by the modern Gael of Argyll. The youthful Somerled, shut up with his father in these native solitudes, brooded over his misfortunes—his soul thirsting to avenge his own and his father's wrongs upon his powerful oppressors. An ancient

* Chron. Meilros.

fragment MS. begins to relate that "Somerled, the son of Gilbert, began to muse on the low condition to which he and his father were reduced, and kept himself at first very retired." An invasion of Morven drew Somerled from his retreat. With a few followers he attacked the Viking aggressors, and drove them to their ships. Encouraged by the display of bravery and successful daring in their youthful leader, Gael and Scot alike flocked to his standard. Morven, Argyll, and Lochaber were successively swept of the Fiongal intruders, and a powerful kingdom was ere long established, with Somerled at its head, who assumed the title of Regulus, or Lord of Argyll.*

Meantime, the Islands of Arran and Bute, which, for three centuries, had continued in possession of the Sudreyjar kings, in tributive subjection to Norway, were wrested from the Norwegians by David I.; and in 1135 they were conferred by treaty on Somerled, and formally annexed to the kingdom of Argyll.†

Whilst the cession of these Islands secured for a time to Scotland the friendly alliance of Somerled, and increased the power and resources of the new kingdom which interposed between the aggressive Norse Jarls and the Scottish Mainland, it still further contributed to deepen the feelings of hostility which existed between the Norsemen of the *outer* Isles and the Skotar-Gaels of Argyll, and occasioned incessant raids and feuds between the two rival kingdoms.

The army of Olave the Red was meanwhile greatly strength-

---

* Gregory's Highlands and Isles, p. 12.
† Skene's Highlands of Scotland, Vol. II., p. 41.

ened by reinforcements from Norway, and Somerled, perceiving his inability to contend with his powerful antagonist, secured the tranquillity and independence of his people by a marriage with Effrica or Rachel, the daughter of Olave, A.D. 1140. The fruits of this marriage were three sons—Dugall, Reginald, and Angus.

Olave died in 1154, after a reign of forty years. He was succeeded by his son, Godred the Black, whose tyrannical government alienated the affections of his subjects, and eventually stirred up a powerful faction under Thorfinn, a Norwegian chief of Man, which had for its object the expulsion of Godred, and the enthronement of Dugall, the eldest son of Somerled, as King of the Isles.

The petty chiefs of the Sudreyjar were readily induced by Thorfinn to join the rebellion, and promise their allegiance to Dugall, whilst Somerled raised a fleet of eighty vessels from Arran, Bute, and Argyll, to depose the Fiongal chief, and reduce the Island of Man. Scarcely had Somerled cleared sight of the Isles, when he observed the dark line of Godred's fleet approaching in the distance,—then the flash of shields and the glistening of arms were reflected on the waters in the pale moonlight. The Gallgael chief, as was his custom, lashed his galleys to those of his Norse foes; then fiercely the battle raged. The clamour of the war-cry, the clash of steel, and the shrill scream of the affrighted sea-fowl, were echoed back in the stillness of night. As morning broke upon the scene of carnage, and victory continued undecided, a truce was declared and a compromise effected between the contending chiefs. Godred ceded to his nephews—the sons of Somerled—

all the South Isles, whilst Somerled agreed to respect the authority of the Fiongal chief over the Island of Man and the Nordreyjar.*

But scarcely two years had elapsed from the date of this treaty when the ambitious Somerled invaded the Isle of Man with a fleet of fifty-three galleys, dethroned Godred, and forced the petty Norwegian chiefs into allegiance.

The possessions and militant resources of Somerled became now so formidable as to disturb the tranquillity, and even threaten the independence of the Scottish kingdom.   The ships of the Gallgael chief swept the west coast of Scotland, and maintained an undisputed supremacy over the whole of the Western Islands, whilst the Kernes and Gallowglasses of Arran and Argyll harried the Scotch and Saxon hamlets within the Highland glens and along the Lowland borders.

In 1153 a treaty was entered into between Somerled and Malcolm the Scottish King, which for centuries afterwards formed an epoch in the charter chronology of Scotland.†

But the faithlessness and continued encroachments of Somerled at last roused Malcolm to the necessity of curbing the ambition and arrogance of his rival neighbour king, and great preparations were made for invading his dominions. Somerled hastened to anticipate the threatened aggression. From the Isle of Man, the Nordreyjar and the Sudreyjar, he assembled a large force, which was further increased by auxiliaries from Norway and Ireland.   The entire flotilla

---

* Chron. Manniæ—Gregory's Highlands and Isles, p. 14.
† Chalmers' Caledonia, Vol. I., p. 626.

consisted of one hundred and sixty galleys, manned and
equipped worthy of the bravest foe,—

> " On each gay deck they might behold
> Lances of steel or crests of gold,
> And hauberks with their burnish'd fold
> That shimmer'd fair and free." *   .

Somerled proceeded up the Frith of Clyde with his
formidable armament—leaving many of his ships stranded
on the shores by the receding tide—till he arrived at Renfrew, where he succeeded in effecting a landing. Scarcely,
however, were his heterogeneous forces formed into battle-
array, than they were furiously assailed by the Scottish army,
under Walter the High Steward. The impetuosity of the
attack threw the invaders into inextricable confusion. After
repeated attempts to regain their position, they were driven
to their ships, leaving their hitherto victorious leader—the
brave Somerled—amongst the slain on the battle-field,
A.D. 1164.†

After the death of Somerled, ‡ the Sudreyjar were divided
between his three sons, Dugall, Reginald, and Angus. Mull,
Tiree, Coll, and Jura fell to the possession of Dugall; Islay
and Kintyre to Reginald; and Bute to Angus, whilst the
Isle of Man reverted to Godred the Black. §

---

* Lord of the Isles.

† Chron. Meilros, 170. Gillecolum, the son of Somerled by a
previous marriage, was also slain.

‡ Somerled is described by an ancient Sennachie as "a well-tempered
man, in body shapely, of a fair, piercing eye, of a middle stature, and
of quick discernment."—*Gregory's Highlands and Isles*, p. 16.

§ Gregory's Highlands and Isles, p. 17.

Arran appears to have been divided between Reginald and Angus, and may have been the occasion of the fierce quarrel which raged between the two brothers. On the death of Angus, who was slain with his three sons by the men of Skye in 1210, the Clyde Islets were seized by his brother Reginald. *

The allegiance of the two Sudreyjar chiefs, Dugall and Reginald, appears to have been equally shared between Norway and Scotland, but repeated attempts were made by the Gallgael to throw off the yoke of their oppressors, and re-establish their independence. A castle was built and forti-fied by Reginald on the Holy Isle in Lamlash Bay,† and from the mountain fastnesses and forest-clad glens of Arran and Argyll, the daring Gallgael made frequent forays into the territories of the Scots.

Reginald survived his brother Dugall, and, according to the Celtic law, succeeded to his possessions. From the former, sprung the MacDonalds of Islay and the MacRuari of Bute; and from the latter, descended the families of Argyll and Lorn.‡

On the death of Reginald,§ Donald, his eldest son, suc-ceeded to Islay, and Ruari to Bute, whilst the Islands pre-

---

* Gregory's Highlands and Isles. Chron. Manniæ.
† New Statistical Account.
‡ Gregory's Highlands and Isles, p. 18.
§ Reginald was one of the most distinguished warriors of these war-like times. He is said to have lived for three years without entering a house where a fire had been kindled, in order to harden his frame for a life of danger and privation.

viously held by Dugall reverted to Reginald's nephews—Dugall, Scrag, and Duncan.

During the reign of Alexander II., strenuous efforts were made for the subjugation of the Western Isles, and their annexation to the kingdom of Scotland; but the Island chiefs were equally unremitting in their struggles, to secure their independence alike of Scottish and Norwegian domination. Whilst Dugall, Scrag, and Duncan endeavoured to shake off the yoke of Norway in Islay and Argyll, Angus * and Ruari fortified and garrisoned the castles of Brodick, Molassa, and Rothesay; and, by forming alliances with the marauding Vikings of the north seas—whose galleys still infested the shores of the Western Islands—they considerably increased their power; defied the authority of the Scottish King; and devastated the lands and hamlets along the shores of the Clyde.

Alexander, the High Steward of Scotland, who had married Jean, granddaughter and heiress of Angus MacSomerled, seized the opportunity which these encroachments afforded him, to invade the Islands of Arran and Bute, and establish his claim to their possession, by right of his marriage with the daughter of their former chief. Whilst the Norwegian power in the Sudreyjar was being threatened by the Scotch, Allan, Earl of Galloway—the daring chief of a lawless and piratical people—invaded and subjugated the Island of Man.†

Olave the Black, the Manx Jarl, fled to Norway, and be-

---

* The Angus Mor of the Sennachies—Son of Donald.

† The Galwegians were at this time virtually independent of Scotland.

sought the assistance of King Haco. "He reported many strong expressions uttered against the Norwegians by the Earl, who hinted that the sea was not more impracticable to Norway, than from Norway to Scotland, and that the Norwegian harbours were not inaccessible to such as would plunder them." Haco, roused by these taunts, despatched Olave with a large armament to reconquer the Island of Man and the Clyde Islets, and to coerce their chiefs into allegiance. Olave arrived safely at Islay, attacked and dispersed the fleet which the sons of Dugall had raised to oppose him, swept the coasts of Islay and Kintyre, and forced many of the Gallgael to join his expedition. After reducing the outer Sudreyjar, Olave sailed up the Clyde, conquered the Island of Arran, and landing in Rothesay Bay, besieged the fortress of Bute. The castle was strongly garrisoned and gallantly defended by the Scotch. From its walls they poured down boiling pitch and lead upon the Norwegians, whose every attack was repulsed by the spears and missiles of the besieged. Olave, therefore, built a covering of boards, beneath which his men fought scathelessly, and with their axes and hauberks proceeded to hew down the walls of the fortress. In three days the castle was razed to the ground, the garrison slain or taken prisoners, and the merciless victors, with their captives and booty, embarked in their galleys, leaving behind them the wasted farms and smoking ruins of the hamlets of Bute.*

---

* Chronicon Manniæ. A Scotch knight, who was taken prisoner, purchased his freedom by the payment of 300 merks of refined silver.— *Bute Inventory*. The B. I. dates the siege in 1226, but it must have been some years later than this.

R

Olave, on his return, succeeded in evading the fleet of Allan, Earl of Galloway, which was prepared to meet him, and after cruising along the coasts of Argyll, he proceeded to Man, and expelled the Galwegians from the Island, whilst the Norwegian fleet sailed northwards, swept the Western Islands, and returned to Norway.

On the departure of the Norse galleys from the Clyde, Alexander, the Scottish King, made overtures to Haco for the purchase of the Western Islands, which were haughtily refused. He therefore resolved to acquire, by force of arms, what he had failed to obtain by strategy. He speedily raised a powerful fleet, which he commanded in person, reduced the inner Hebrides—Arran, Bute, and the Cumbraes—and expelled the Norwegians whom Olave had left to retain possession of them. After rounding the Mull of Kintyre, he sailed northwards, in order to invade Angus in his native stronghold, and coerce him into tributive allegiance to the Scottish crown; but on his arrival at Kerrara, a little Island near the coast of Mull, Alexander was seized with a fever, of which he died on the 8th July, 1249.*

Alexander III. was no less strenuous than his father in his endeavours to annex the Western Islands to Scotland. Whilst the Earl of Ross devastated the Northern Hebrides, the Scottish King compelled the chiefs of the Sudreyjar to acknowledge his supremacy.

Meantime, Ruari and the Gallgael chiefs who had been dispossessed of their lands, fled to Norway, and informed Haco of the cruelties and aggressive measures of the Scotch.

* Fordun, lib. ix. c. 63.

The Norwegian King made immediate preparations for the reconquering of the Hebrides and the invading of Scotland. He embarked with a powerful fleet; and arriving at Ronolds-voe,* in the Shetlands, he strengthened his armament by levies from the Isles and the Mainland. Thence, sailing southwards, Haco forced the Island chiefs to join his expedition, and being met by Magnus, King of Man, with the Manx fleet, he found himself at the head of an armament of two hundred galleys.† Everything promised favourably for the success of the Norwegians. Their long dark galleys, with their gilded dragon prows, flung their shadows on the clear surface of the ocean mirror; and spears, and swords, and burnished shields, gleamed and flashed in the autumn sunlight. The songs of the scalds floated about in the still twilight, broken by a thousand echoes from island cliffs and mountain glens, stirring the hearts of the brave Norsemen with the fierce lusts of conquest and glory, and inciting them to rival the daring deeds of the heroes of Walhalla.

Whilst the Norwegian fleet lay at anchor off the little Island of Gigha, Haco despatched five of his galleys, under Ruari, to subjugate the Clyde Islets, and fifty more to devastate the coasts of Kintyre. Ruari besieged and took the castles of Arran and Bute, and plundered the Islands. On the submission of Angus—the Regulus of Arran and Kintyre—the ships sent to lay waste his possessions were

---

* Haco arrived at Ronoldsvoe on 7th July, 1263. The date has been ascertained by an annular eclipse of the sun, mentioned by the King's Scald in his account of the expedition.

† Haco's Expedition.

recalled, but a thousand stirks and bullocks from the hills
of Arran and Argyll were demanded by Haco as the tribute
of his allegiance.*

Haco now rounded Kintyre with his fleet, anchored in
Kilbrannan Sound, and proceeded to assemble his land forces
in the Island of Arran.† On receiving messages from the
Scottish King with a treaty of peace, a truce was declared.
Alexander offered to cede to Norway the whole of the
Western Islands conquered by Magnus Barefoot in 1093,
excepting the Clyde Islets—Arran, Bute, and the Cumbraes—
over which he claimed the right of Scotland's supremacy.
But the unconditional surrender of the whole of the Hebrides,
Nordreyjar and Sudreyjar, would alone satisfy the ambitious
demands of the Norwegian King, and confident in the strength
of his armament, he proceeded to enforce his claims by invading the Scottish Mainland.‡

Magnus, King of Man, was despatched with sixty ships to
devastate the shores of Loch Long—Skipafjordr. Arriving
at the head of the Loch, as Sturla relates, "the persevering,
shielded warriors of the thrower of the whizzing spear drew
their boats across the broad isthmus. Our fearless troops,
the exactors of contribution, with flaming brands wasted the
populous Islands in the lake, and the mansions around its
circling bays."§

Whilst Haco with his fleet bore down upon the Ayrshire

---

* Haco's Expedition; Gregory's Highlands and Isles; Worsaee's
Danes and Norwegians.

† New Statistical Account.   ‡ Haco's Expedition, pp. 14-19.

§ Loch Lomond—Lokulofni.

coast,[*] the dark clouds which had hung heavily over the summits of Goatfell and Ben Ghnuis crept in murky folds athwart the heavens, portending an approaching tempest. Ere long the rising wind began to whistle through the cordage of the Norwegian galleys, and the crested waves to break in sheets of foam against their dragon prows, till their oaken timbers creaked, and the stout hearts of the Norsemen quaked with fear. Ten of Haco's ships were wrecked on the shores of Loch Long. Others were torn from their moorings off the Cumbrae Isle, and driven ashore near Largs. A superstitious dread seized the minds of the Norsemen:—" Our sovereign," says Sturla, " encountered the horrid power of enchantment, and the abominations of an impious race. A tempest, magic raised, blew upon our warriors ambitious of conquest, and against the floating habitations of the brave. The roaring billows dashed shielded companies on the Scottish strand."[†]

Meantime the army of the Scottish King was seen approaching along the heights behind the little hamlet of Largs—1500 knights and barons mounted on fleet Spanish chargers, and a numerous force of foot soldiers armed with

---

[*] At this time "the accounts of the Sheriff of Ayr contain a note of the expenses of the master gunner, Balistarius, with his two watchmen and porter in the King's Castle of Ayr; the expense of repairing the castle itself; a payment of messengers who thrice went as spies on the King of Norway; wages to the watchers of the King's ships for twenty-three weeks; three dozen of bow-staves; and the price of oatmeal, wheat, cows, salt, and wine for the garrison."—*Scotland in the Middle Ages*, p. 123.

[†] Haco's Expedition.

bows and spears, commanded by the High Steward of Scotland—under the King in person.

About 900 of the Norwegians succeeded in effecting a landing near Largs; 200 of these occupied a neighbouring height, but on the advance of the Scottish army, they were driven from their position. Their retreat threw the Norwegian reserve into disorder. In vain the followers of Haco endeavoured to rally and defend themselves behind their shattered galleys. A few put off in their ships, but were engulfed in the surf; others fled along the shore, but were pursued, overtaken, and slain. The timely arrival of reinforcements from the fleet secured a temporary advantage over the Scots. Their King was wounded in the face by an arrow, and Alexander, the High Steward, was slain; but the discomfited Norsemen were in turn speedily forced to retreat and trust their safety to their tempest-tossed galleys.

As the storm continued to rage with unabated fury, no further attempts were made to hazard another landing. A truce was granted to the Norwegians to bury their dead. Over the slain the sepulchral mound was raised to the mournful chant of the bards, and the wailing of the wind in the neighbouring wood.*

Haco thereafter proceeded to collect the remains of his once noble armament, and, sailing down the Frith, anchored in Lamlash Bay, where he lay for a few days to repair his shattered galleys.† He thence rounded the Mull of Kintyre,

---

* Haco's Expedition.

† Haco is said to have bestowed Arran at this time on a chief, named Margad. It was whilst lying in Lamlash Bay that Ivar Holm, the old comrade of Haco, died.—*Haco's Expedition.*

and proceeding northwards, reached the Orkneys on 29th October. There the heart-broken King died six weeks afterwards, with the chronicles of his ancestors sounding in his ears, and was buried in the grand old church of Saint Magnus, in Kirkwall.*

On the death of Haco, the Hebrides were swept by a powerful fleet, and the submission of the Insular chiefs to Scotland for a time effectually enforced.

In 1266 a treaty was concluded with Hakonson, King of Norway, by which the entire Western Islands were ceded to Scotland for the payment of 4000 marks sterling, and a yearly tribute of 100 marks.† The Clyde Islands were thereupon confirmed in the possession of James, son of Alexander, High Steward of Scotland.

The traces of Norwegian occupation are less remarkable in the southern than in the northern Hebrides.

In Mull, Lewis, Harris, Skye, etc., not only are Scandinavian names of places abundant, but the peculiar Norse type of features is frequently to be met with amongst the inhabitants, who also possess all the old Norse Viking's love of the sea, which heaves and surges around their Island coasts.

In Kintyre, and the Islands of Colonsay, Oransay, Jura, and Islay, Scandinavian etymons are less numerous, but sufficiently so, to indicate the former existence of a considerable Norwegian colonisation. In Islay, the Il of the Sagas— which is said to be named after Yula, a Danish princess,

* Torfæus' History of Norway, IV., 343.
† There is a transcript of the treaty in a very old MS. in the Register House, Edinburgh.

who lies buried beneath two large monoliths in Knock Bay *
—there is a terraced mound similar to the celebrated Thing
or Tynwald Hill in the Isle of Man, where the Manx Kings
held their courts of justice in the halcyon days of Norse
supremacy.   Many old traditions, too, of the Norwegian
Vikings still linger about these Islands; and spears, and
swords, and Danish axes have been dug up from their mossy
beds in the glens and moorlands, by the native agricul-
turalist.

The Inner Sudreyjar—Arran, Bute, and the Cumbraes—
from their contiguity to the Scottish mainland, were chiefly
inhabited by the Scotch or Skotar-Gaels, who, as we have
seen, frequently attempted to shake off the galling yoke of
their Norwegian oppressors.

In Arran, a few Scandinavian etymons exist in the names
of the bays and estuaries of the Island, where the Viking
rovers found a safe harbourage for their galleys, and an easy
ingress to their plundering forays—hence, Brodick or Broad-
wick,† Soor*dale*,‡ Glenash*dale*, Glais*ter*,§ Lochranza,‖ and
Goat*fell*.¶ It is probable, too, that the derivation of *Whiting*
—Whiting Bay—in spite of the popular notion, is of purely
Scandinavian origin.   Near the southern extremity of the
Bay, at the entrance to Glenashdale, there is a hill known as
Knocklecarleu—Consultation Hill—where the ancient inhabi-

---

* Worsaee's Danes and Norwegians in Scotland.
† Wick—Dan, Creek, or Bay.   ‡ Dale or *daill*—a valley.
                    § Ster-*stadr*—a place.
‖ A-Ey-Island—Lochranza—The Loch of Arran's Isle.
                ¶ Fell-fjall—a rocky mountain.

tauts are said to have held their deliberation meetings in times of threatened invasion.* By the Norsemen these hills were known as Tings or Things—hence Whiting—and from the Tynwald of the Bay, the Norse Jarls could watch the movements of their Scotch and Saxon foes on the Lowland coast.

The impress of Norwegian domination in Bute is now almost entirely effaced, and scarce a vestige remains of the bold Viking mercenaries, who held their revels in the old Castle of Rothesay during the sovereignty of Somerled and Ruari; whilst the Norwegian name of the Cumbrae Isles —*Kumreyar*—seems to indicate that they were inhabited chiefly by the Cimri or Gaels.†

The civilisation of the inhabitants of the Sudreyjar, during the Norwegian supremacy, was not less advanced than that of their Scotch and Saxon neighbours. Their ships were similar to the long galleys of the Norsemen—built with successive banks of oars—and many of them sufficiently large to carry several hundred men.‡ They possessed a considerable fleet of these long galleys, with which they swept the Frith of Clyde, invaded the fiords of the Saxon coasts, and intercepted the richly-freighted sloops of the Guild-brethren monks. Arran, Islay, and Argyll were the emporiums of these plundering raids and daring piracies. The

---

* Headrick's Arran, p. 103.

† Worsaee's Danes and Norwegians, p. 277.

‡ Haco's ship was built entirely of oak, contained twenty-seven banks of oars, and was ornamented with richly-carved dragons overlaid with gold.

wine and the spices, which were the exclusive luxuries of the nobility and privileged monks of the Scottish Mainland, were oftentimes the common fare of the petty Island chiefs in their rude strongholds, whilst the Skotar-Viking lover adorned his bride with the silken robes, the chains, and brooches, and bracelets, of which he had despoiled the Saxon maid in her southern home.

But though the Skotar-Vikings of the Isles were ever ready to enrich themselves at the expense of their neighbours, they were not the less industrious in the cultivation of their lands, and possessed undisputed excellence in the practice of many useful and ornamental arts. A poet of the North, in describing a dress unusually gorgeous in its fabric and colour, adds—that it was spun by the Sudreyjar.* Angus is styled by Sturla—"the distributor of the beauteous ornaments of the hand;" and the inhabitants of Bute are described as "the forlorn wearers of rings." Even in science and literature, they obtained no inconsiderable distinction.† The sons of the chiefs received their education with the favoured Saxon youth in the schools and monasteries of Ireland, and the numerous remains of oratories and chapels throughout the Isles and Western Highlands testify to the zeal and fidelity of the Gallgael Christian teachers.

The history of the Norwegians in the Isles is chequered by many a cruel raid and lawless aggression. Smoking hamlets, wasted lands, and desecrated churches, were left in the track

---

* Johnstone's Lodbrokar—Stanza XV.
† Macpherson's Illustrations of Scottish History, under word "Ilis."

of their forays and conquests; but whilst our hearts freeze with horror as we contemplate the cruelties, oppressions, and devastations entailed by these merciless sons of Odin, our breasts heave with the warm glow of admiration as we think of their indomitable energy, their unflinching bravery, and the manly independence of their character.

CHAPTER II.

Castles.

"Full in the midst, a mighty pile arose,
  Where iron-grated gates their strength oppose
  To each invading step; and strong and steep
  The battled walls arose, the fosse sunk deep.
  Slow round the fortress roll'd the sluggish stream,
  And high in middle air the warders' turrets gleam."

PRIOR to the seventeenth century, the sword was the charter, and the stronghold the confirmatory grant of the lands and fermes of the lawless chieftains of the Highlands and Islands of Scotland; and hence it is that the few historical notices we possess of Arran, after the departure of the Norsemen, are chiefly connected with its Castles and Peels, around which the waves of neighbouring aggression surged and broke, leaving in their wane the wreck of ruined walls and wasted fields.

The old castles and fortalices of the Western Highlands are characterised by the massive solidity and rude simplicity of their construction. They generally consisted of three to four stories. The lower story was used as a dungeon, the second as a guard-room for the garrison, and the third contained the grand-hall, were dwelt the baron, or the keeper, and his family; whilst the rude war-engines of the times were bristling from the topmost battlements.

The Peel, or Bastle-house of the petty chief, owed its security more to the natural advantages of its situation, than to the architectural sufficiency of its defences. Like the Baronial Castle, the most prominent and important part of the building was the doujon or keep. The apartments were placed one above another, with a long narrow stairway communicating with each, which could be easily defended against attack by a few bold catherans; whilst scattered around, were the rude cots of the vassals or retainers of the chief, who were ever ready to rally around him in times of danger.

Situated upon some coastland eminence, with the sea-fowl screaming around their gray towers, and the surf beating against their base, or rising from some rocky islet, imbedded in mountain tarn, or inaccessible Lowland morass, these old feudal strongholds were usually places of great strength, and oftentimes of impregnable security.

Though the Islands and Highlands of Scotland may not vie with England in the number and magnificence of their castellated ruins, we have good reason to believe that ere their coasts and borders were swept by civil strife and Southern foe, they possessed numerous fortified buildings, and these of no mean architectural pretensions. During the protracted and disastrous struggle for the Scottish crown, one hundred and thirty-seven castles, fortalices, and towers were razed to the ground by King Robert the Bruce, who taught his people to trust for protection to the woods, the morasses, and the mountain fastnesses of their country, rather than to stone walls and garrisons;* and many a Lochmaben, Dunbar, and Caerlaverock may have reared their formidable buttresses along the rocky cliffs of our Island coasts, and within our Highland glens, of which no vestige now remains.

No Island of the West had more need of its Castles and Peels, than the little Island of Arran, in those troublous times of Scottish history. Situated on the very confines of feudal strife, and commanding the entrance to the Frith of Clyde, its glens and its bays were frequently swept by neighbouring raid and foreign invasion. But the brave spirit of the Gallgael beat in the hearts of the Arran men; and when the descendants of those roving-loving Skotar-Vikings of Islay and Argyll sought to harry the shores of their Island home, they armed themselves for defence, and fortified the castles around their coast; and so the Brandani of Arran and Bute arose, with all the traditional daring of their ancestors, to meet and oppose the lawless Kernes and Gallow-glasses of the rebel Island Lords.

The good Dean of the Isles—Donald Monro—writing about Arran towards the middle of the sixteenth century, says:— "Herein are thre castils,—ane callit Braizay, pertaining to the Earle of Arrane; ane uther auld hoose callit the castil of the heid of Lochrenasay, pertaining likewise to the said Earle, and the third callit Castil Donnain, pertaining to ane of the Stuarts of Bute's bluid." †

---

* Fordun, Book XII., chap. x.   Appendix, Note X.
   † Description of Western Isles.

Brodick Castle[*]

is situated towards the north side of Brodick Bay. Its
turrets alone are seen from sea or shore, peering from amidst
luxuriant clumps of beech and fir, and bathed in the gray
shadows of Ben Ghaioul, whose rugged peaks, swathed in
mountain mist, tower behind in grand magnificence.

About 1306, it is noticed as "ane stith castell of stane."[†]
Towards the end of the eighteenth century it is thus described:—"The castle is built in an oblong form; from south
to north there is a wall of two stories high that encompasses
the castle and tower; the space within the wall, on the south
side the castle, is capable of mustering a battalion of men.
The castle is four stories high, and has a tower of great
height joined to the north side; and that has a bastion close
to it, to which a lower bastion is added. The south and
west sides are surrounded by a broad wet ditch, but the east
and west sides do not admit of a wet ditch. The gate looks
to the east."[‡]

Since Martin wrote, the castle has undergone considerable
alterations and additions. The rude massive bastion, with
its parapet and embrasures built by Cromwell on the north-
east side of the building, still remains; but towards the south,
facing the bay, a new tower was erected a few years ago,

---

[*] Brethwic—Brathwik—Brethwik—Brathwic—Bradewik—Braizay
—Brodick.

[†] The Brus—Spalding Club.

[‡] Martin's Western Islands, pp. 222, 223.

containing the principal entrance, with a magnificent oaken balustrade communicating from the hall to the upper apartments.

The grounds surrounding the castle have been tastefully remodelled. A forest of old trees and young saplings extends behind, beyond the park, whilst in front, and nearest the bay, there is a terraced lawn of the richest emerald, studded with clumps of evergreens, and chequered with *parterres* of the rarest exotics, which luxuriate here as in the soil of their own sunny climes.

The old castle is believed to date its origin from a circular fortlet of the early Islanders, which is said to have occupied the site of the present building,* but neither tradition nor history helps us to discover by whom the primitive fortlet was demolished, or at what period the castle of "Brethwic" was built.

About the middle of the twelfth century Somerled the Great is said to have built a fortress on the Holy Island,† which, with the castle of Rothesay, in Bute, formed the outguards of the insular possessions of the Norwegians, prior to the final cession of these Islands to Scotland by Haco in 1263.

The Island of Arran, with its commanding situation, its extent, and the fine natural harbours which indent its shores, must have been a place of considerable importance in these early times, and it is probable that ere Somerled had built the fortress of Melansey, the castle of Brodick was protecting the *wick*, with the little galley fleet of the Viking Islanders moored along its beach.

* New Statistical Account.   † Ibid.

During the invasion of Haco, the castle was reduced by the Norwegians,* but it appears to have been soon after rebuilt by James, the High Steward of Scotland, who received possession of the Island of Arran on the death of his father.

Towards the end of the thirteenth century the High Steward appears to have conferred the lordship of Arran and the governorship of Brodick Castle on his kinsman, Sir John Monteith—whose brother was at this time warden of the castle of Rothesay, under Edward I.† Blind Harry thus refers to him:—

> "Sir John Monteith was then of Arran lord,
> To Wallace came and made a plain record,
> With witness there by his oath he him band,
> Lawty to keep to Wallace and Scotland."‡

The people of Arran were staunch adherents of Wallace and Bruce during the wars with England:—

> "Good westland men of Arran and Rauchlie,
> Fra they be warned they will all come to me,"

exclaimed Wallace when encouraging his followers; and not in vain. The Brandani of Arran and Bute flocked around the standard of Sir John Stewart—the nephew of Monteith—on the field of Falkirk, their tall, athletic frames exciting

* Aikman's History of Scotland, Vol. I., p. 380.
† Rotuli Scotiæ, Vol. I., pp. 31, 32.
‡ Blind Harry's Wallace, B. VII., p. 188. Though we have given this quotation from Blind Harry, we by no means uphold him as an authority.

the admiration of their enemies; and when their brave leader fell in the conflict, their heaped-up bodies formed a wall around his bleeding corpse.

But Sir John Monteith never forgave Wallace for securing his own retreat from that disastrous field, without attempting the rescue of Stewart, and his feelings of animosity and revenge culminated in the seizure and delivery of the Scottish patriot to his English foes:—

> " A thousand thre hundyr, and the fyft yere,
> Efter the byrth of our Lord dere,
> Schyre Jon of Menteth, in tha dayis,
> Tuk in Glasco Willame Walays."*

During the sanguinary struggle for Scottish independence, the castle of Brodick was alternately held by the English and Scotch. Immediately after the battle of Falkirk, an adventurer from Ireland—Thomas Bisset—landed in Brodick Bay with a large body of troops, took possession of the Island, and received permission from Edward to retain it in the name of England.† In 1306, Sir John Hastings was governor of the castle with his "squyers and yeomanrie."‡ At this time Bruce, with his small but faithful band of adherents, was shut up within the little Elba of Rathlin. The gallant Douglas, weary of inactivity, and impatient to make one more effort to free his country from English thraldom, thus addressed the King:—

---

* Winton, Vol. II., p. 130.   † Hemingford, T. I., p. 166.
‡ The Brus, XXXII.

Brodick Castle.

"I have heard say that in Arrane,
In a strong castle made of stane,
An Englishman that with strong hand
Holds the lordship of that land."

Sir James Douglas and Sir Robert Boyd requested and received permission from Bruce to pass over to Arran. Ere the evening mists were gathering around the hills, they landed with a few followers in the lovely Bay of Ranza; and after drawing their galleys ashore, and concealing their oars and tackle within the rank brushwood of the Glen, they started on their journey across the Island. With the stars alone to guide them, they treaded wearily and warily over hill and moor, through tarny brake and mountain morass, till surmounting the heathery *string*, they arrived in Glen Cloy, and encamped there, within the old fortress of the early Islanders.

"So that ere day was drawen light,
They were embusht the castle near—
Armed upon the best manner."*

The same morning Douglas, who had climbed the summit of a neighbouring hill, to survey the position of the castle, observed three galleys enter the Bay. He immediately called together his men; hurried down to the beach; surprised the under-warden of the castle as he was proceeding to land their cargoes—which consisted of provisions, arms, and clothing for the garrison; slew about forty of the escort, and secured the stores. The noise alarmed the "squyers and yeomanrie"

* The Brus, XXXII.

of the castle, who issued forth to the rescue; but they were met and defeated by Douglas, and those who escaped were driven within its walls. Douglas and his men, loaded with spoil, threaded their way through the dense copsewood, to their retreat in the glen, where they "made right merrie" over the English cheer.

A few days after this, Bruce himself landed in Loch-Ranza with the remnant of his followers, in thirty-three galleys. On inquiring at a young woman whom he met if any strangers were in the Island, he was conducted towards the place of their concealment; but Douglas and Boyd, on the King's arrival, were hunting in the neighbouring wood. The meeting of Bruce with his friends is thus quaintly and touchingly told by Barbour:—

> "The king then blew his horn on high,
> And gert his men that were him by
> Hold them still, and all privy;
> And syne again his horn blew he.
> James of Douglas heard him blow,
> And at the last alone 'gan know,
> And said, 'Soothly yon is the king;
> I know long while since his blowing.'
> The third time therewithall he blew,
> And then Sir Robert Boid it knew;
> And said, 'Yon is the king, but dread,
> Go we forth till him, better speed.'
> Then went they till the king in hye,
> And him inclined courteously;
> And blithly welcomed them the king,
> And was joyful of their meeting,
> And kissed them; and speared syne
> How they had fared in hunting?
> And they told him all, but lesing;

> Syne laud they God of their meeting.
> Syne with the king till his harbourye
> Went both joyfu' and jolly."*

Soon after his arrival in Arran, Bruce appears to have besieged and taken the castle of Brodick, and from its turrets he is said to have watched for the concerted fire on the Turnberry coast, which the faithful Cuthbert was to light, should any hope exist of striking a blow for Scotland's freedom. As the old ballad has it:—

> "When day gaed doon ower Goatfell grim,
>   And darkness mantled a',
> A kingly form strode to and fro
>   On Brodick's Castle wa'.
>
> "And aye he gazed ayont the Frith,
>   Where blasts were roarin' snell,
> And aft he leaned upon his sword,
>   Sad, muttering to himsel'.
>
> "'In vain, in vain,' at length he cried,
>   And hung his head in woe,
> When, streaming far through storm and gloom,
>   He saw the beacon flow."†

Preparations were immediately made for embarking.

> "The Bruce's followers crowd the shore,
> And boats and barges some unmoor,
> Some raise the sail, some seize the oar.
> Their eyes oft turned, where glimmered far
> What might have seemed an early star
> On heaven's blue arch."‡

---

* Brus XXXIII.; Pennant, Vol. II., p. 171.
† Macdonald's Days at the Coast, pp. 163, 164.
‡ Scott's Lord of the Isles, Canto V.

And so—

> "The noble king,
> With his flote and a few menzie,
> Three hundred, I trow, they might be,
> Went to the sea out of Arran."*

Tradition still lingers fondly over the places in Arran associated with the name of Bruce.† Towards the base of the Drumidoon cliff, are the caves where he is said to have resided when in the Island, before taking the castle, and there is a little rocky promontory near Whiting Bay, with its memorial standing-stone, whence he is supposed to have embarked for the Carrick shore. Near the same spot is said to have stood the rude Highland cot, where the repeated attempts of the spider to weave its tiny web, from beam to rafter, taught him perseverance and hope; and his faithful hostess, ere he left the hut, brought him her two sons to aid his enterprise, and predicted

> "How his purpos suld tak ending."‡

In the old tower of the castle, too, there is a rude deal table, drilled by moths, and seamed with age, around which the royal exile and his trusty friends were wont to sit and quaff their wine, drinking revenge to Scotland's foes. §

Sir John Monteith, Lord of Arran, was won over by the clemency and generosity of Bruce.‖ The King not only

---

* Barbour's Bruce, p. 89.

† King's-cross; Dalry—King's Plain; Tor-an-righ—King's Mount; King's Cove.

‡ The Brus, XXXV.   § Local tradition.

‖ When keeper of the castle of Dumbartonshire—which he held under Edward—Monteith formed a scheme for the capture of Bruce. The plot, however, was discovered, and after a short imprisonment, Monteith received the royal pardon.—*Irving's Dumbartonshire.*

confirmed him in his former possessions, but, in 1310, gave him a grant of Knapdale;* and no one fought more bravely or did better service for the cause of Scotland on the bloody field of Bannockburn, than the betrayer of the patriot Wallace. His name appears amongst the signatures to the celebrated letter of vindication to the Pope, anno 1320, where he is styled *"custos comitatus de Menteith."*

In after years, when the good King Robert was living in retirement on the banks of the Clyde, after he had succeeded in working out the independence of his country, he occasionally visited his old friend, Sir John, in his castle of Bradewik, and carried off from the Island, for the supply of his royal larder at Cardross, many of its stirks and bullocks. In 1326, there is entered in the Chamberlain's accounts the sum of two shillings paid to six men for passing over to Arran with a ship to the king;† and in 1329, the year of Bruce's death, the Chamberlain accounts for forty-seven marts of the stock of Arran, counting four "stirks" for one mart, received from Ingeram of Colchone.‡

Sir John Monteith was succeeded by his second son of the same name, in the lordship of Arran and governorship of Brodick Castle.§

This Sir John was a good friend to the monks of Kilwinning, upon whom he conferred the dues, rents, and fees, pertaining to the churches and chapels of Arran, and long after

---

* MS. quoted in New Statistical Account.
† Compota Camerar, Vol. I., p. 7.   ‡ Ibid, p. 82.
§ Argyle Inventory.

his death the grateful fathers performed masses for his soul's behest within the old monastery of Saint Winning.*

On the accession of Robert, son of Marjory Bruce and Walter, sixth High Steward, to the throne of Scotland, the Island of Arran, with its castles, became the patrimony of the crown; and its inhabitants having taken up arms in support of their master, they were freed from the annual tribute of grain, which they had formerly paid, and received many other important privileges.

It is generally believed that the Fullertons, Cooks, Stewarts, Hunters, and others, who are said to have held lands in the Island subsequent to this period, received their charters from King Robert the Bruce; but as Bruce had no possessions in Arran, this tradition is manifestly at fault. The only existing charter of these grants is that held by the descendants of M'Lewis,† and as this charter is signed by Robert II., in the second year of his reign, it is probable that the other petty chiefs received their titles from the same king, in compensation for the services above noticed.

The sheriffship of Arran and Bute was shortly after this conferred by Robert II. on his natural son, John Stewart, known as the Black Stewart, from his dark complexion.‡ By his marriage with Jean, daughter of Sir John Semple of Eliotstone, Stewart had three sons, of whom William Stewart, his second son, was keeper of Brodick Castle from 1445 to

* Rob. Index, Vol. III., pp. 419, 434.
† New Statistical Account.
‡ Bute Inventory.   Crawford's Renfrewshire.

1450, for which he received a yearly salary of £20, in addition to the revenues of certain crown lands in the Island.*

About this time Arran was repeatedly invaded and overrun by "those cursed invaders from Kintyre." To prevent their landing, the castles of Brodick, Lochranza, and Kildonan were fortified and garrisoned, and a little navy of galleys, manned by the vassals of the chiefs, floated about within the bays and around the coasts of the Island, but in spite of every vigilance and precaution, raids were made, lands laid waste, and cattle pillaged.

In 1455 the castle was razed to the ground by Donald Balloch of Islay. Instigated by James, Earl of Douglas, these arch-rebels, the Earl of Ross and the Lord of the Isles, entered into an alliance which had for its object the subversion of the Scottish throne.† An armament was fitted out, consisting of five hundred galleys belonging to the Lord of the Isles, manned by five thousand of his vassals, under the command of Donald Balloch. Though the expedition failed to disturb the independence of Scotland, it was most disastrous in its results to the Islets of the Clyde. A cotemporary chronicle relates that " there were slain of good men fifteen, of women two or three, of children three or four. The plunder included five hundred or six hundred horses, ten thousand

---

* Compota Camerar, Vol. III., pp. 419, 434. In 1445 Niel Jamieson, chamberlain of Bute, disbursed 26s for thirteen dozen of cod bought from the fishermen of Arran for the King's use; and £4 10s for the hire of a galley and expenses of the boatmen for *twenty* days in conveying them from Arran to Dunbretane.—*Comp. Cam.*, *Vol. III.*, p. 421.

† Gregory's Highlands and Isles, p. 198.

U

oxen and kine, and more than one thousand sheep and goats. At same time they burnt down several mansions at Innerkip around the church, harried all Arran, stormed and levelled with the ground the castle of Brodick, and wasted with fire and sword the Islands of the Cumbraes. They also levied tribute upon Bute, carrying away one hundred bolls of malt, one hundred marts, and a hundred marks of silver."*

Shortly after this, the Island of Arran, with its castle of Bradewik, passed into the possession of the Boyd family. Robert, Lord Boyd, a man of consummate craft and unbounded ambition, succeeded in raising himself, by means of his office of High Justiciar of Scotland, to a position pre-eminent in power and state. In 1465 he was appointed Ambassador to England; and the following year he was constituted Regent, during the minority of James III., and entrusted with the guardianship of the young King, with his brothers and sisters. This trust he improved to his own advantage, by marrying his eldest son and heir, Sir Thomas Boyd, to the Princess Mary, the King's eldest sister, the bridegroom receiving the Island and Earldom of Arran as a dowry.

The young Earl, however, was not destined long to enjoy his honours. Whilst absent in Norway, where he was employed as one of the ambassadors in completing the arrangements towards an alliance between James III. and Margaret, daughter of the King of Norway, the jealousy and hostility of the nobility, induced by the haughty rule of his father, burst forth. Disgraced at court, slighted and shunned by

* Auchinleck Chronicle, p. 55.

the King, the old Regent's ruin was complete. The Earl of
Arran, warned by his faithful wife, on his arrival in the
Forth, fled to the Continent, where he soon afterwards died.
His titles were conferred upon the eldest son of the Scottish monarch, whilst the lands of Kilmarnock, and others
forfeited by his father, Lord Boyd, were bestowed upon her
Majesty, the Queen of James III., during her life, "for her
robes, and to supply her with the ornaments of her head-
dress."*

In 1488 James IV. granted to Hugh, third Lord of Montgomery, certain "fermes" of Arran, with the keeping of the
"old place and castle of Bradewik," and further appointed
him Justiciar within the Islands of Arran and Bute.†

Towards the beginning of the sixteenth century, Brodick
Castle fell into the possession of the Hamilton family. In
1503, James Lord Hamilton,—whose father had increased
his influence at court by his marriage with the King's sister,—
the widow of Sir Thomas Boyd, Earl of Arran—so distinguished himself by feats of strength and valour at Holyrood
during the rejoicings attending the King's marriage, that he
was created on the spot Earl of Arran, and implemented with
the crown lands of the Island and the castle of Brodick.‡

In 1526, George Tait is mentioned as having been appointed captain of the castle by the Earl.§

About two years after this, during the sanguinary feuds
which raged between the clans of Argyll and M'Lean, the

* Acta. Parl. Vol. II., p. 187.
† Reg. Mag. Sig., lib. xii. No. 60.
‡ Reg. Sec. Sig., Vol. II., ff. 102, 132.   § Kilmichael Charters.

castle was burned down, and the lands around the Bay laid waste.[*]

It was of too much importance, however, in those lawless times—situated as it was on the confines of Island and Highland feudalism—long to remain in ruins, so it was speedily rebuilt, it is said by James V.,[†] who repeatedly visited the Western Isles in person, for the purpose of forcing the turbulent chiefs into submission. Whilst returning from one of these expeditions in 1540, the King landed in Arran, and passed a few days in Brodick Castle.[‡] Nicolay d'Arfeville, cosmographer to the King of France, has left us the following description of the garb worn by the Arran men when King James visited the Island:—"They wear, like the Irish, a large and full shirt, coloured with saffron; and over this a garment, hanging to the knee, of thick wool, after the manner of a cassock. They go with bare heads, and allow their hair to grow very long; and they wear neither stockings nor shoes, except some who have buskins, made in a very old fashion, which come as high as their knees."[§]   This is the same old Highland dress worn by the men of the Isles when King Magnus invaded the Sudreyjar in the eleventh century.

After the death of James V., the castle was razed to the ground by the Earl of Lennox. In order to coerce the Scottish nation into a treaty of marriage between his son Edward, Prince of Wales, and the young Queen Mary,

* Pitcairn's Criminal Trials, Vol. I., p. 139.
† Pennant, Vol. II., p. 172.
‡ Gregory's Highlands and Isles, pp. 147, 148.
§ "La Navigation du Roy d'Ecosse," etc., published in Paris in 1583.

Henry VIII. fitted out an expedition under Lennox, who had espoused the English cause. Lennox, who was actuated by feelings of the deepest hostility towards the Earl of Arran, entered the Clyde with a considerable fleet, besieged and demolished the Castle of Brodick; plundered the Island, and, after taking formal possession of it in the name of England, delivered it over, according to agreement, to Sir Rise Mansell, an English knight, who accompanied the expedition. On the defeat of Lennox, however, Mansell hastily abandoned his prize.*

The rebuilding of the castle was scarcely completed, when the Island was laid waste by the English, under the Earl of Sussex.†

Meantime the increasing influence at court of the Hamilton family had excited the enmity of the nobility, and in 1579, at the instigation of the Earls of Morton and Angus, they were stript of their possessions and titles. The keeper of Brodick Castle at first refused to betray his trust, even at the command of the King; but, convinced of the hopelessness of resistance after the flight of his chief, and the capitulation of Hamilton Castle by its governor, Arthur Hamilton of Merton, he agreed to the proffered conditions of surrender. The following letter, addressed by King James VI. to Colin, sixth Earl of Argyll, appears amongst the "Argyll Papers:"

"MAI 13, 1579.

"Rycht traist cousing and counsalour. We greit you heartly weill.

* Gregory's Highlands and Isles, p. 164.   † Ibid, p. 198.

"Understanding the Kepars of the house of Brydik in
Arrane to be willing to rander the same, thair lyffis saulf for
the cryme of dissobedience of our charge to render the said
house and castell; We will you thairfore in our name to
grant them the said condicioun, letting them depart with
ther awin propre baggage, saulffiing the munitioun and
victuallis being within the said house and castell, whilk ye
sall caus ressaue upon Inventair, and be preservit to our use.
Placeing our servitour Niniane Stewart as Keipar of the said
house and all things ressauit thairin, quhill the farther
knawledge of our mynd and plesure.

"Thus we commit you to God, &^{c.}

"JAMES R."

The confiscated estates of the Hamiltons were distributed
amongst the favourites of the young King, whilst the Island
of Arran, and the title of Earl of Arran, were conferred upon
Captain James Stewart, son of Lord Ochiltree, a man in-
famous for his profligacy, cruelty, and ambition. He was
mainly instrumental in the execution of the Earl of Morton,
in which was supposed to be fulfilled a somewhat obscure,
though well-known prophecy of Merlin's.   It runs thus:—

> " In the mouth of Arran an selcouth shall fall,
> Two bloody harts shall be taken with a false train,
> And derfly dung doun without any done;
> Ireland, Orkney, and other lands may,
> For the death of those two, great dule shall make."

Morton, being a Douglas, bore the bleeding hart on his

coat armorial, and the "mouth of Arran," it was conjectured, referred to Captain Stewart, Earl of Arran.*

But even the King could no longer shield his favourite from the vengeance of the nobility, and in 1585 the Earl was disgraced, and denounced as a traitor, whereupon his lands and titles reverted to their former owners.

On the restoration of the Hamiltons, Niniane Stewart† was succeeded in the custodianship of Brodick Castle by Patrick Hamilton, brother of the Laird of Preston. A right bold, fearless man was this Patrick Hamilton. In 1587, he was outlawed for not appearing before King and Council, to answer a complaint of one Abacuck Bissett, a Writer to the Signet in Edinburgh. Bissett, a man of "quirks and quibbles," had offered Hamilton some provocation during the sitting of Parliament in the church of Saint Giles. The hasty captain drew his sword, and according to Abacuck, "cut off the haill fingers of his left hand."‡

We next find the governorship of the castle in the hands of Paul Hamilton—whose grave may be seen within the old chapel of Kilbride—probably the son of the preceding. On the rebellion of the Clan Donald in 1615, Paul received a commission from Government to keep the Island clear of the rebels.§

During the wars between Charles and his Parliament, the Earl of Arran espoused the cause of the King, and the Castle

* Domestic Annals of Scotland, Vol. I., p. 146.
† Son of James Stewart, Chamberlain of Bute.
‡ Domestic Annals of Scotland, pp. 180, 181.
§ Record of Privy Council, 8th to 22d June, 1615.

of Brodick was seized and retained alternately by the Royal
and Covenanting parties. Whilst the Earl of Strafford was
about to depart with an expedition, in 1639, to reduce the
turbulent and establish the cause of royalty throughout the
West of Scotland, the Earl of Arran, for his encouragement,
desired him to touch at his Island of Arran, assuring him of
the assistance· of "all his naked rogues there." Strafford's
designs were, however, anticipated by the Covenanters, and
Argyll, with a force of 900 men, swept the west coast, landed
in Arran, and took possession of its castle from the "naked
rogues" of the Earl, without striking a blow. Pending the
temporary cessation of hostilities, the castle was delivered up
to the Marquis' retainers; and, in 1644, a dukedom was conferred upon Hamilton by King Charles, for his faithful and
valuable services.

On the subsequent defeat of the King's supporters, the
Island was invaded, and the castle seized and garrisoned by
Cromwell; and, a few weeks after the execution of Charles,
the unfortunate Duke of Hamilton shared the same fate as
his royal master. Cromwell, as we have seen, built a massive
quadrangular tower or bastion towards the north-east side of
the castle, which still exists. The retainers of the Duke, in
Arran, exasperated at the loss of their chief, and offended by
the attentions bestowed on their wives and daughters by the
rude soldiers of the Protector, surprised the garrison while
out on a foraging expedition, chased them around the shore
towards Sannox, where they were overtaken and slain. The
stone from beneath which the last survivor was dragged and
dirked is still shown by the roadside.

James, Duke of Hamilton, was succeeded by his brother William, Earl of Lanark, who was mortally wounded at Worcester in 1651, and the Island of Arran, (with the exception of a few farms) and the old castle of Brodick, have since remained in the possession of his descendants.

The stringent measures enforced by Government after the battle of Culloden in 1745, to suppress the raids and feuds of the lawless Highland and Island chiefs, succeeded at last in securing protection and tranquillity to the people of Arran; and after this period little of interest is known in connection with the castle.

It was the residence of the present Emperor of the French in 1847, when on a visit to his cousin, the Princess Marie of Baden, now Duchess of Hamilton; and, during the "shooting season," it is the *habitat* of His Grace the Duke of Hamilton.

Of the old fortress, however, so often demolished and rebuilt, not a stone now remains, save the ruined tower, built by "old Noll" two centuries ago.

But our steps still linger about the castle, as our thoughts dwell upon its venerable pedigree and chequered history; and so, before leaving it, we pass within its walls. Ascending the grand staircase, we enter a large hall. Its ceilings are ornate with the intricacies of heraldic devices, and its walls are hung with old paintings, large life-size portraits, in their thick massive frames, of men and women who have acted their part on this world's stage, and passed away. Fair ladies are there, in long silken robes, with forms and features cast in Nature's fairest mould; and stately knights are there, and steel-clad warriors, descendants of the Mellant Jarls who came

v

over with the Conqueror from Normandy—men brave of heart and large of limb, who fought and bled in many a bloody field for king and country. As we gaze around, and dream of these bygone times of feud and strife, of ladies fair and warriors grim, there seems a breathing life beyond the painter's art in these old portraits.

We pass from out the castle's gate, and tread our way over the emerald sward, between flowery *parterres* and clumps of evergreens down to the golden beach. The sun has flung a flood of sheen over the purple sides of Glen Cloy, lighting up the sequestered corrie, where the ruins of the old fortlet lie half buried amidst fern and heath. Around the bay, the shore is streaked and dotted with the little village cots. The serrated ridge of Ben Ghaioul is clearly defined against the azure sky, and the castle, within its protecting shadow, nestles amidst the greenest foliage.

Hill and glen, and bay and castle, are all bathed in the romance of old associations. The raven-pennon, from dragon-prowed galleys, seems again to wave defiance within the Bradewik; or the rolling waves, lashed into clouds of spray by the rising hurricane, strew the beach with the wreck of Haco's proud flotilla. And then, with the glow of patriotism, we think of that bravest King of Caledon, treading the castle's turret walls, and gazing wistfully into the hazy darkness for the concerted signal fire on the Carrick coast. Or our thoughts turn to later times, when raid and strife laid waste the fields and lands within the Island, and the village huts around the bay, and the old castle itself, were heaps of smoking ruins.

Kildonan Castle.

Kildonan Castle.*

PERCHED on the edge of a low precipitous cliff of trap, which stretches out in the form of a vein or dike, from the south-eastern extremity of Arran to the little green Islet of Pladda, is the skeleton Peel of Kildonan. Like most of the baronial castlelets of the Highlands and Isles, it consists of a quadrangular tower of four stories. Its walls are five feet in thickness, built of slate and sandstone, the coarse mortar cement encrusted by the shells of the whilk and limpet from the shore. The apartments are small and gloomy, with arched roofs, and narrow loop-hole windows, without a vestige of architectural adornment. The rich foliage of the ivy tree now clothes the dismantled walls, and the tall grass and the graceful fronds of the fern, cover the floor of the grand-hall, with an emerald carpeting.

The castle is somewhat meagre in historical interest. It is supposed to have been built by Alexander II. as one of a line of towers extending from the mouth of the Clyde to Dumbarton;† but the style of the building refers to a somewhat later period—probably to those rude times of war and strife when Scotland was struggling with the Edwards for its independence.

The High Steward of Scotland, as we have seen, held un-

* Kildaunane—Kildonane—Kildonnan—Castle-Donnan—Kildonan.
† There are the ruins of an old building on the Ailsa rock, bearing a striking resemblance to the ruined Peel of Kildonan.

divided possession of Arran after it was abandoned by the Norwegian Jarls; and the Peel of Kildonan may have been built by one of his successors as a watchtower from which to signal the alarm of an invasion to the Stewart's men of Bute and Strathclyde.

Several enactments were passed by the Scottish Kings for the regulation of these watchtowers. When the rumour of Donald Balloch's expedition reached the Government, the Peels of the Clyde were placed in a state of defence, and piles of faggots were collected within the turrets ready for the torch when the galleys of the enemy appeared in the distance. And these were the signals:—"Ane baile is warning of their cumming, quhat power that ever they bie of; twa bailes togidder at anis they are cumming indeed; four bailes ilk ane beside uther, and all at anis as foure candelles, suithfast knawledge that they are of great and meanis far." *

Kildonan was a royal castle until 1405, when it was granted by King Robert III. to John Stewart of Ardgowan, along with the lands of Kildonan, the three Largis, the two Keskedelis, Clachlane, Glenasdasdale, the Twafurlangis, and the Dupennylandis.† This John Stewart, of whom Sir John Maxwell Stewart of Blackhall is the lineal descendant, was a natural son—*filius naturalis*—of Robert III. From his dark complexion, he was known as the "Black Stewart."‡

In 1472, his grandson, James Stewart of Ardgowan and Kildonan, received a charter from King James III. of the

---

* Acta Parl. Scot.   † Bute Inventory.

‡ Crawford's Renfrewshire.

"Crownership of Arane, on the resignation of that office by John MaKclowy—MacLewis—of Killemichel."* He was married to Margaret, daughter of Lord Lyle, and was succeeded in his estates by his son and heir, John Stewart, who received a confirmatory grant from James IV. in favour of himself and Janet Kennedy, his wife, of the Tenpennylands of the Island. This grant embraced the castle of Kildonan, and all the lands conferred on the Black Stewart by Robert III.†

In exchange for certain possessions in Perthshire, John Stewart conveyed the Tenpennylands of Arran, in 1503, to Ninian Stewart, who at this time was Sheriff of Arran and Bute, proprietor of Corrigills, and governor of Rothesay Castle. ‡ This charter was confirmed by King James IV.§ Ninian was third in descent from John Stewart, natural son of King Robert II. John received from his father considerable possessions in Arran and Bute; and, in a confirmatory charter from Robert III., he is styled *"dilecto fratri suo."* ‖

In 1539 James Stewart was served heir to his father, Ninian Stewart, in the lands of Corrigills, the Tenpennylands, and the Sheriffship of Arran and Bute.¶ When Monro visited Arran in 1549, "Mr James" was proprietor of Kildonan Castle. "He and his bluid," says the Dean,

---

* Reg. Mag. Sig., lib. vii., No. 273. We have here, and elsewhere, given the authorities and the name of places as they appear in the "Origines Parochiales."
† Crawford's Renfrewshire.
‡ Bute Inventory. § Reg. Sec. Sig., Vol. II., fol. 130.
‖ Bute Inventory. ¶ Ibid.

"are the best men in that countrey." * But whilst the good Dean was eulogizing the "bluid" of the Stewarts, their chief was being summoned before Parliament on the crime of treason, for assisting the Earl of Lennox, in 1544, in devastating the Islands of Arran and Bute, and demolishing the old castle of Brodick. The charge appears to have been secretly abetted by the Earl of Arran, then Regent of Scotland, and ultimately led to the forced surrender by Stewart of all his lands in Arran, and their transfer to James Macdonald of Dunivaig.

The cruel raids of the Island Lords were at this time the terror of the lairds and barons of the mainland. Secure in their native fastnesses, they defied the law and authority of Scotland, and were frequently the mercenary allies of "our auld enemies of Ingland." Macdonald of Dunivaig, however, appears to have rendered valuable assistance to Argyll in repelling the invasion of Lennox in 1544, for which he received several grants of land from Queen Mary.† In 1547 he joined the English interest, and in a letter addressed to the Lord Deputy of Ireland, he craves his Lordship to send to his aid a fleet and army "to the Yll of Sanday, besyid Kintyer, at Sanct Patrikis day next to cowm," for the purpose of making a foray on the Scottish borders. ‡

To win over this fickle but powerful chief, the Earl of Arran bound himself to "forfeit the Sheriff," and infeft Macdonald in his lands. But Stewart received a remission from

---

* Description of the Western Isles.
† Reg. Mag. Sig. XXIX., No. 118.
‡ State Papers, Vol. III., p. 548.

Queen Mary for his treasonable doings, and the designs of the intriguing Regent were frustrated. Meantime Macdonald, Shylock-like, became clamorous for the fulfilment of the bond, and the Earl, driven to extremities, coerced the timid Stewart by entreaties and threats into a sale of his castle and lands, for which he agreed to pay 4000 marks; to infeft the Sheriff in the £10 lands of Cumbrae, and to reconcile him to the Sheriff of Argyll. This sale included the Tenpennylands already enumerated, the castle of Kildonan, the lands of Tonreddir, and the "Isle of Pladow, with the towers, mills, fishings, and other pertinents." * The sole reservation made by Stewart was the lands of Corrigills and the sheriffship of Arran, which continued in the possession of his descendants.†

Macdonald had not been long in Arran when his grasping ambition and petty aggressionary measures excited the jealousy and animosity of the neighbouring lairds, and induced the Earl to devise means for removing him from the Island. From his brother, the Bishop of Argyll, he purchased, in 1556, the manor or castle of Saddel in Kintyre, with the lands adjoining, in consideration of £1200 paid him for various purposes, and £10,000 paid to meet the tax granted to the Queen. These the Earl offered to Macdonald in exchange for his Arran possessions. The offer was accepted, Macdonald binding himself to keep open house for the Earl and Bishop, and to do nothing to the prejudice of the Island of Arran. And so the rude "kernes" of the

* Bute Inventory. † Ibid.

Dunivaig lord left the old castle of Kildonan, and entrenched themselves within the "fortalice of Saddagall."[*]

On the forfeiture of the Hamilton estates, the castle and lands of Kildonan were granted to Archibald Stewart of Largizean, in whose hands they remained till the restoration of their previous owners.[†]　They appear, however, to have again reverted to the Stewarts of Bute.　When Headrick visited Arran towards the beginning of the present century, the Marquis of Bute was proprietor of Kildonan Castle, from whom it was lately purchased, along with the adjoining lands and those of East and West Corrigills, by the Duke of Hamilton.[‡]

𝕷𝖔𝖈𝖍𝖗𝖆𝖓𝖟𝖆 𝕮𝖆𝖘𝖙𝖑𝖊.[§]

THERE are few places in Arran so rich in the picturesqueness of their scenery, or in the interest of their traditional and archæological associations, as the Loch of Arran's Isle and its surrounding neighbourhood.　The green ridges buttressing in the bay, the dark ravine of Eis-na-barradh opening inland, the white cots of the Clachan dotting the beach, and the ruined Peel in the centre, form a group worthy of the pencil of a Turner.

---

[*] Collect. de Rob. Alb., pp. 88, 89.

[†] Bute Inventory.　　　　　[‡] New Statistical Account.

[§] Lochede—Locharanesay—Locheraynsay—Lochrenasay—Lochranza.

The pen of Scott has thus sketched the scene, but it is only a faint picture of the original:—

"The sun, ere yet he sunk behind
Ben-Ghoil, 'the mountain of the wind,'
Gave his grim peaks a greeting kind,
    And bade Loch Ranza smile.

. . . .

Each puny wave in diamonds roll'd
O'er the calm deep, where hues of gold
    With azure strove and green.
The hill, the vale, the tree, the tower,
Glow'd with the tints of evening's hour,
    The beach was silver sheen." *

The castle stands upon a green peninsula, which stretches across the bay, forming an outer and inner bason. It consists of two square towers united, apparently the work of different periods. The walls are thick and massive, cemented by a coarse gravelly mortar, and pierced by a few small loop-hole windows. The entrance is on the west, and conducts into the guard-room, which again communicates with the dungeon; whilst the grand hall, and the battlements above, are reached by a narrow, dark stairway, dimly lighted by a solitary arrow-cleft opening. The keeper's hall is a small gloomy apartment, about twelve feet square, with a fire-place large enough to roast an ox.

Like the old Peel of Kildonan, the "ane auld hoose" of Lochranza is now ruined and roofless; but a few centuries ago, when its walls were entire, and its little delta site was

---

* Lord of the Isles, Canto IV.
W

perchance a sea-girt Islet, it must have been a place of great strength and security, and may have withstood many a raid of the Island Lords when the castle of Brodick was in ruins.

The castle is said to have been built by one of the Stewart Kings as a hunting-seat.* It is mentioned by Fordun, *circa* A.D. 1400, as one of two royal castles in Arran.†

Shortly after this it appears to have been held by John de Menteith, Lord of Arran, who, in 1433, conferred it, along with the adjoining lands, and those of Clachilan, Kilbryde, Blairmore, and others, on Sir Duncan Campbell of Lochaw.‡ Sir Duncan Campbell, of whom the Duke of Argyll is the lineal descendant, was married to a daughter of John Stewart of Ardgowan; and, in 1445, he was raised to the dignity of a Lord of Parliament, by King James II.§

Reginald M'Alexander—Ronald M'Alister—is noticed between 1445 and 1450 as keeper of Lochranza Castle, and tenant of the crown lands of Lochede, Tonregethy, Achagallane, Catagil, Pennerevach, Altgowlach, Machirbeg, and Machremore, the yearly dues of which amounted to £16 6s 8d, and twelve bolls of beer, but which Ronald refused to pay on account of his farms having been laid waste during the invasion of Arran by Donald Balloch of Islay.||

The Castle, with the lands of Lochranza, Catthaydill, the two Turregcys, Tymoquhare, Dugarre, and Penreoche, was thereupon granted by King James II. to Alexander, Lord Montgomery.¶

* New Statistical Account.   † Scotichronicon, lib. ii., c. 10.
        ‡ Argyle Inventory.   § Burke's Peerage.
|| Compota Camerar, Vol. III.   ¶ Reg. Mag. Sig., lib. iv., No. 282.

Alexander was succeeded by his grandson, Hugh, Lord Montgomery, who, in 1488, was keeper of the castle of Brodick, and in 1489 of Rothesay Castle, for which he received a yearly salary of 40 marks.* By attaching himself to the interests of James IV., he was raised to the dignity of Earl of Eglinton. During the feud which raged between the families of Eglinton and Glencairn, the mansion of Eglinton was demolished, and the family charters and papers destroyed; but, in 1528, the Earl received a new charter of the castle and lands of Lochranza from King James V.†

Great preparations were made about this time by the Scottish Government for invading the Isles, and reducing their turbulent chiefs to subjection. In August, 1529, Sir John Campbell of Calder requested, on behalf of his brother, the Earl of Argyll, that the householders along the shores of the Clyde should be commanded to meet him at Lochranza Castle, with provisions for twenty days, thence to make a descent on the Kintyre coast. On account of the harvest, however, this project was abandoned.‡

In 1614 the castle was again fortified and garrisoned, and the bay chosen as the *carn-a-whin*, or rendezvous, for an attack on the clan Donald.§

About the middle of the seventeenth century, Lochranza was in the possession of Alexander, the sixth Earl of Eglinton; who was succeeded in 1661 by his son and heir, Hugh, Earl of Eglinton, in the castle and lands of Lochede, Lochranza, and Sannox. Whilst the castle of Brodick was garri-

---

* Reg. Mag. Sig., lib. xii., No. 115.   † Ibid, lib. xxii., No. 207.
‡ Gregory's Highlands and Isles, pp. 131, 132.   § Ibid.

soned by the Parliamentary troops, and his own mansion of Ardrossan razed to the ground by Cromwell, the Earl was forced to conceal himself, with his family, in the little Cumbrae Isle.*

The next notice we can find of the castle is in 1685, when James, Lord Montgomery of Skelmorlie, received a grant of the lands of Lochranza and Sannox. He was succeeded, in 1696, by his son Robert, Lord Montgomery, in the same lands.†

Some time after this, the castle, and the farms in Arran held by the Montgomeries of Skelmorlie, passed "in wadsett" into the hands of the family of Hamilton, in whose possession they now remain.‡

Lamlash Castle.

THERE is the vestige of a square tower near the Whitehouse in Lamlash Bay. The foundation-stones are alone traceable beneath the rich verdure of the lawn; but their extent sufficiently indicates the former strength and importance of the building.

Tradition is the sole historian of the castle of Lamlash; but that such a castle existed is extremely probable. When the bays of Brodick and Lochranza, and the headland of

---

* Crawford's History of Renfrewshire.   † Ibid.
‡ New Statistical Account.

Kildonan, and the little Holy Isle, were commanded by their peels or towers, it is not to be supposed that the excellent harbourage of Lamlash, where Haco moored his flotilla after his defeat at Largs, would be left defenceless.

It is said that the stream which enters the bay to the south of the village, at one time flowed north of the Whitehouse, and that the ships which sought the harbour were wont to anchor beneath the castle walls.*

---

* An anchor was dug up, some years ago, from the former bed of the Lamlash stream, a few yards from the site of the old building.

CHAPTER III.

"I do love these ancient ruins.
We never tread upon them, but we set
Our foot upon some reverend history."

THE introduction of Christianity into Britain was even more important in its results than the diffusion of the Metallurgic Arts or the Roman Invasion.

Among the distant Islets of the Hebrides, and within the glens and mountain retreats of Caleydon, where the Roman Eagle had scarce dared to penetrate, the banner of the Cross was borne by a few zealous missionaries, and the rude and warlike Britons were constrained to acknowledge the Divine potence of the Christian faith.

During the third century, the persecutions of Diocletian in the East had driven many Christian converts to the British Isles; and ere the Roman legionaries had been withdrawn to protect the Capitol from the invasion of the Goth, the son of a British prince had visited Rome, and received a commission from Pope Circius, A.D. 384, to preach the Christian faith among the heathen tribes of North Britain. The zealous Saint Ninian built his *Candida Case* on the sea coast at

Kilbride Chapel, Lamlash.

Withern, in Galloway*—the shrine of many a pious pilgrimage in later times. The good Saint died, A.D. 432, the year
before Saint Patrick was sent on his mission to Ireland by
Pope Celeste. But there succeeded him many other devoted
missionaries—St Palladius, St Rule, St Woloc, St Kieran,
and St Kentigern, until, in 563, St Columba landed with a
few disciples on the surf-beaten Islet of Hii, or Iona—the Ii
Cholum Chille,† and there he built his church of wattle-
work, and taught his missionaries, and sent them forth to
teach and to preach throughout the Western Islands and
Scottish Mainland.‡

The early pioneers of Christianity secured the confidence
of the Britons by respecting their old customs and heathen
rites, and gradually succeeded in weaning their affections
from the creed of their fathers, by grafting its outward
ceremonies and superstitions upon the simple formula of the
Christian faith.

The gray monolith, beneath which slept the ashes of the
British hero, was sculptured with the Cross. The Christian
Church was built beside the revered stone circle. The
springs and the mountain streamlets which had been worshipped with Druidic rites, were consecrated by the Christian
teachers, and converts to the new religion flocked to the
holy wells to drink their healing waters. The smoke which

---

* Bede, 1, 3, c. 4.

† The Island of St Columba's Cell. It received the name of Ithou
from the Scotch—hence Iona.

‡ The remains of the cells of the Scoti-Irish Saints have also been
found in the North of Europe.

ascended from the funeral-pile was no longer seen hovering over the ashes of the hero-chief—nor cairn, nor barrow, nor cromlech was raised over the *cistvæn* or cinerary urn; but beneath the shadow of the Christian fane, a stone, with sword and cross sculptured upon it, rested upon the warrior's grave.

Before leaving their native shores, the Scoti-Irish had received the blessing of St Patrick, and were accompanied in their expedition to Argyll in 503 by their faithful Christian teachers. A century afterwards the light from Iona shed its rays over the heathen darkness of Caleydon; and the numerous remains of primitive chapels and cells within the Scottish glens, and along the shorelands of the Western Islands, attest the zeal and persevering assiduity of the followers and successors of St Columba. In the parish of Rothesay, in Bute, there may be traced the ruins of twelve chapels; in Harris, fifteen to twenty; and in many of the barren and deserted Islets of the Hebrides, now tenanted alone by the sea-fowl and the ptarmigan, we find the ruined walls of the early Christian oratories.*

St Columba superintended personally his charges in the Isles, and he is believed to have occasionally resided in Arran, whilst visiting his faithful disciple St Molios, who laboured in the Island. There once stood a cairn or mound in Glen Suidhe, known as *Suidhe Challum Chille*, where St Columba is said to have sat and refreshed himself with his disciple, whilst travelling from Lamlash to the little chapel at Shiskin.

---

* New Statistical Account.

St Molios,* as we have seen, lived in a sea-worn cave in the Island of Lamlash, thereafter called the Isle a Molass, or Holy Isle. Tradition relates that he officiated alternately at Lamlash and Shiskin, and died at the advanced age of one hundred and twenty. His tombstone is pointed out in the old church-yard of the Clachan.

The traditional account of St Molios, however, differs somewhat from that contained in the "*Acta Sanctorum,*"† where his history is sketched with all the minuteness of date and detail which characterises the legendary narratives of the Irish hagiography. He is said to have been born in Ireland, A.D. 566, about three years after St Columba arrived in Scotland. His eagerness and aptitude for instruction induced his uncle, St Blane, to undertake his instruction, and in the little Island of Bute, the young student spent his boyhood days, reading and translating the Scriptures in the chapel of Kingarth; or from the summit of Dun-na-Goil watching the clouds gathering around the peaks of Arran, and the waves breaking in foam against the Cumbrae Isles. After receiving the rudiments of his education in Bute, St Molios returned to Ireland. At the early age of twenty, he again visited Scotland, and for several years lived the life of a hermit in one of the Western Isles—supposed to be the Islet of Lamlash. In 614 he was appointed to the Abbacy of Leighlin in Ireland, and afterwards raised to the dignity of a Bishop and Apostolic Legate to the Church in Ireland.‡

* St Molios—Molingus—Macljos—Molios—Servant of Jesus.
† Bolandist's Collection.
‡ Bryce's Arran, p. 141, on the authority of John M'Kinlay, Esq.

X

The hermitage of the Saint was, for centuries after his death, the favourite shrine of pilgrims from the Isles and Mainland, who have left their initials and holographs scratched over its sandstone roof.

The progress of Christianity in the southern Hebrides was for a time retarded by the arrival of the Norse rovers. These lawless Vikings, imbued with the fierce, blood-thirsty spirit of their gods—the terrible Odin and Thor—swept the Western Islands in their long-oared galleys, harried the hamlets and lands around their coasts, and plundered and burned the chapels of the Culdee missionaries. Again and again the little island fortress of Christianity—the Isle of St Columba— was invaded and despoiled, its monasteries sacked, and the devoted monks put to the sword.*

But the light of Christian truth ere long prevailed over the darkness of pagan superstition and barbarism. The monasteries and chapels were rebuilt, new converts were made, and new lands visited and Christianised.†

No sooner had the Norsemen begun to colonise the Islands they had conquered, than they, too, were gradually brought under the influence of the Christian faith. The raven-pennon was stript from their galleys and replaced with the banner of the Cross. Chapels and monasteries were respected and protected, and the Viking chief was no longer interred beneath the *Skibssœtninger* by the shore, but found a grave within the hallowed precincts of the Christian church.

* Annals of Ulster.

† When the Northmen visited Iceland, in the ninth century, they found the crosiers, books, and bells of the Irish monks.

But though the Norsemen of the Isles had ceased to aspire after the pleasures of the Walhalla, they were Christians but in name. Now and again the Viking leader would turn pious pilgrim, and visit the Holy Land in his old age, but more frequently his Christianity was borne and enforced at the point of the sword.

The Bishopric of the Isles, founded in 838, was united to the diocese of Man on the conquest of the Sudreyjar by Magnus Barefoot in 1093.* It was probably through the influence of Nicholas, the Manx Bishop, whose name appears cut in the roof of St Molios' Cave, that Reginald MacSomerled, *Rex Insularum*, founded a monastery on the Islet of Lamlash—the Holy Isle—towards the end of the twelfth century. The monastery was situated on the north-west side of the Island, and appears to have been subject to the Cistercian monastery of Kintyre, where the body of Somerled was buried.

It was a common usage in monkish times to confer the smaller chapels or cells, with their fees, tithes, and altar-offerings, upon the religious houses of the Regulars,† and frequently certain lands and pecuniary gifts were connected with these grants. In accordance with this custom, Reginald supplemented the monastery of the Holy Isle with the lands of Lamlash, Shiskin, Benan, and Torlin, in Arran, and *unum denarium ex qualibet domo.*‡ This grant was confirmed in

---

* In 1334 the Island of Man was seized by the English; and in 1380 the united diocese of Man and the Sudreyjar was dissolved, and the Scotch thereafter chose their own Bishop for the Isles.—*Keith's Bishops.*

† Paisley had thirty parish churches, Holyrood twenty-seven, and Melrose and Kelso as many.

‡ Reg. Mag. Sig., lib. xiv., No. 408. Chart of Paisley, p. 377.

1508 by King James IV., in favour of David, Bishop of
Argyll; and these, and the other possessions enjoyed by the
good monks of Saddel, were thereupon erected into the
"Barony of Sagadul." *

During the "visitation" of Dean Monro to the Holy Island
in 1594, the old monastery was "decayit," but for many
generations the grounds adjoining were used as a burial-
place by the people of Arran. Not a vestige of ruined wall
or gravestone now remains. About eighty years ago, a
boat was overturned whilst conveying a funeral party
from Lamlash to the Island, by which several people were
drowned. The burying-place was thereafter abandoned,
and in 1835 the tombstones were removed, and a crop of
onions and carrots was raised over the graves of the dead.†
An aged hawthorn now extends its leafless branches over
the site of the monastery, built by the son of the mighty
Somerled.

On leaving the graves of their fathers on the Holy Isle,
the inhabitants of Arran looked around for another place to
bury their dead, when, lo! a bright gleam of light was seen
flickering amongst the trees, where nestled the little chapel
of Kilbride. This they regarded as a Divine signal, and the
church-yard was thereafter chosen as their principal burying-
place.‡

The old "paroch kirk" of Kilbride§ is situated to the

---

* Reg. Mag. Sig., lib. xiv., No. 408, 481.
† New Statistical Account.   ‡ Local tradition.
§ Ecclesia Sancte Brigide—Saint Brigid Kirk. Kylbrid—Kilbride
—Mark-na heglish (Blæu's map). It is probable that, at one period,

north-west of Lamlash Bay. It is one of those rude and primitive, but picturesque ruins, which, though barren of architectural interest, heightens the charm of Highland scenery by the associations of olden times with which it is invested. Its massive, unchiselled walls, with their small arched doors and windows, and the general features of the building, indicate a venerable antiquity. It is now roofless. A stately ash rears its gnarled trunk within the sacred walls; and a rowan-tree has wriggled its way through the chinks of the southern gable, shaking the old ruin with every blast of wind. From north to south, the building is intersected by a modern fence, which partitions, on the east, a small cell or chamber, a few feet square, paved with gravestones. The western division contains two door-ways—the one on the south was the principal entrance to the church, the other, on the north, was wont to be opened on baptismal occasions for the escape of the fiend, but at all other times carefully closed. Near the door, and built into the northern wall, are the font and pesino. The "doctrine of regions" exerted a strong influence over the minds of the Scottish people, and to the present day, there exists in Arran a lingering remnant of this old superstition. The tombstones of many generations surround the ruined chapel of Kilbride, but not a grave was opened to the north of the building, until the ground to the south was quick with human dust.*

Arran formed one parish. In 1294, a charter of Alexander of Hyle is witnessed by Marice, the *Vicar of Arran*, and, in 1326, Sir Benedict is noticed as *Rector of Arran.—Origines Parochiales.*

* The south was held sacred to things heavenly and Divine.

We have carefully searched amongst the tall grass for ancient sculptured stones, but though a few remain worthy of description, many of the most interesting have been almost entirely effaced by the tread of visitors.

Near the entrance to the church-yard, there is a horizontal slab, with a floral cross and a long two-handed sword carved upon it—probably the monument of a knight or esquire. There is an adjacent stone rudely shaped, bearing the effigy of a kilted Highlander, with sword by his side. Tradition has attached a tragic interest to this old gravestone. The story runs thus:—There were two lairds or petty chiefs in Arran—the one called Walter Fion, the fair-haired; the other Duncan Tait. These men were sworn friends and inseparable companions. A mischief-maker, of the name of M'Nish, wagered that he could alienate their affection, and change their friendship into mortal hatred. Meeting Fion on a certain day, M'Nish told him that the friend in whom he so fondly confided had conceived a great enmity towards him; that he was secretly aspersing his character, and only waited the opportunity to take his life. The same villanous lie was told the unsuspecting Tait, and as implicitly believed. Next morning the two friends met on the shore a little to the north of Lamlash. Without explanation, they drew their swords, and, in the fierce struggle for revenge, they were both slain. They were buried in one grave—distinguished by this primitive sculptured-stone.*

An adjoining slab bears the representation of a shield and sword, the symbols of a knight or man-at-arms.

* Local tradition.

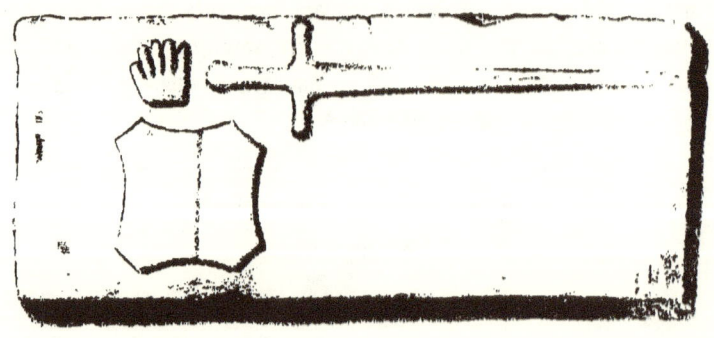

Within the chapel we discovered a cruciform head-stone. Another was found a few years ago beneath the ruins of the chapel, and is now placed over the grave of a Catholic sailor-boy who was washed ashore in Lamlash Bay. These pillar crosses were introduced about the middle of the eleventh century.* They are generally rudely chiselled, and exhibit the first deviation from the unhewn monolith of the early Britons.

Among the enactments made in the reign of King Æthelred, A.D. 994, is the following:—"It hath been an ancient custom, in this country, to bring the dead often within the churches, and thus to make cemeteries of those places which have been consecrated to the worship of God. Now we desire that from henceforward no man be buried in the church, unless he be of the sacerdotal order, or, at least, a holy layman; so that it be known that by the sanctity of his life, he deserved to have his body buried there." †

This privilege, however, appears to have been more freely and widely conceded in later times. Within the little partitioned cell on the east side of Kilbride Chapel, the floor is paved with gravestones, many of which are apparently of great antiquity. Since 1763 the Fullertons of Kilmichael have been buried here. There is the stone of John Fullerton—who died in 1784—with this quaint epitaph traced upon it:—

"This was the man, who free from toil and strife,
In his own ground did pass his peaceful life."

* Manual of Sepulchral Slabs and Crosses, pp. 47–49.
† Ibid, p. 16.

Another has the following inscription:—

Hear lays
Pal Hamilton
Captain of Arran
P H   M H
P H   E H
Patrick Hamilton of Coats
his son
16———64

Beside the Captain's grave there is a slab upon which we can with difficulty decipher—

Here lyes
Nugent Kerr, son to Robert Kerr,
Director of
His Majesty's Chancellary
of Scotland
15 April 1747

A stone, with a cross and sword elegantly sculptured upon it in bas-relief, may also be seen. It is in excellent preservation. The cross and its shaft are formed of the beautiful floral and knot-work ornamentation which so strikingly resembles the illuminated letters of the ancient Irish and Anglo-Saxon MSS. The sides of the stone are adorned by a trailing floral stem of graceful design.

Some years ago the eastern gable of the chapel fell into ruins, and from amongst the stones a small square block of freestone was picked up, upon which are carved an elegant monogram, the date 1618, and a ducal coronet. It was no doubt a presentation to the Church by the Marquis of Hamilton, who was at this time patron of Kilbride and its

Stones in Kilbride Church Yard.

chapels; and the scriptural homily *Fir God*, carved beneath the initials of his Lordship's titles,* may have been oftentimes pointed to, by the reverend pastor in persuading the rude Islanders to a life of peace and godliness. On the reconstruction of the gable, this interesting stone was built into the wall, where it may now be seen partially concealed by the leaves of an ivy tree, which mantle the old building.

The earliest record we can find of Kilbride Chapel occurs in 1357, when Sir John Menteith—Lord of Arran—granted to the monks of Kilwinning the advowson of the churches of St Bride and St Mary, with their chapels and pertinents. This grant was afterwards confirmed by David II.

The King's confirmatory charter may be worthy of translation. It runs thus:—"To all the children of the blessed Mother Church now living, or yet to be born, who may see or hear these present writings, read:—

"John of Menteith, Lord of Arran and of Knapdale. Health in the Lord for ever. Know that I, for the good of my soul, and that of Katherine my late wife, and for the good of the souls of our ancestors and successors, have given, granted, and, by this present charter of mine, confirmed to God, and the blessed Virgin Mary, to good Wynnyn, and to the monastery of Kylvynnyne in Conyngham, to the abbots and monks there worshipping God, and to those who will worship him there for ever, the right of presentation and patronage

---

* These were:—Marquis of Hamilton; Earl of Arran and Cambridge; Lord Even, Innerdail, and Aberbrothok.

of the churches of St Mary and St Bride, in the Island of Arran, with their chapels, and with all other properties which to the said churches, with their chapels and lands, by right belong, or may ever in future come in any manner to belong, to be held and possessed by the said monastery and monks for ever, with all rights belonging to them, in free, simple, and perpetual alms." *

These grants were again confirmed by King Robert III.†

In 1452, the crown lands of Kilbride and Kilmorie, yielding an annual rental of £56 18s 8d, were conferred by James II. on the Canons of Glasgow, in compensation for the sum of 800 marks, lent to the King out of the offerings of St Mungo.‡

It is not known how or when these grants passed out of the hands of the Monks of Kilwinning and the Canons of Glasgow. It is probable, however, that the patronage of the chapels was conferred by James IV. on James, Lord Hamilton, along with the crown lands and Earldom of Arran, as, in 1540, James, Earl of Arran, was *confirmed* by James V. in the advowson of Kilbride.§

The present church of Kilbride, situated towards the south end of Lamlash, was built in 1773, but the burial-place surrounding the old "paroch kirk" is still used by the Islanders.‖

The prebendary chapels referred to in the preceding

---

* Reg. Mag. Sig., p. 34.   Robertson's Index, p. 49.
† Robertson's Index, p. 145.   ‡ Reg. Mag. Sig., lib. iv., No. 268.
§ Reg. Sec. Sig., Vol. II., p. 102.   ‖ New Statistical Account.

charter, are those of South Sannox, Glen Cloy, and Glen-ashdale.

The first of these was situated near the entrance to Glen Sannox. It has been long since removed, but the church-yard still exists, surrounded by a modern wall, into which is built the rudely-carved image of St Michael—the patron saint.

Not a vestige remains of the little cell in Glen Cloy. It also was dedicated to St Michael, who appears to have been a favourite Saint with the Arran people in Popish times.

A few minutes' walk along the margin of the Ashdale stream, and we arrive at the old burying-place and chapel of the Glen. The former is a mere cairn-like mound, dotted over with rude, unhewn slabs and boulders. But Nature has done more than man could do to adorn the simple graves of the Islanders. The golden hues of the furze, the purple tints of the heath flowers, and the graceful leaves of the fern, chequer the heaving turf with a mantle of the richest beauty. Some ancient silver coins were found in one of the graves.* The ruined walls of the adjacent chapel are the remains of a building about ten by twelve feet. It was probably the votive offering of some pious laird or chief to the mother church of Kilbride.

The old Parish Church of Kilmorie † stood on the farm of Benicarrygan. The foundation-stones, which are the sole

---

* Now Statistical Account.

† Kilmure—Ecclesia Sancte Marie de Arane—Kilmory—Kilmore—Kilmorie.

remains of St Mary's Cell, represent a building about nineteen feet in length by ten in breadth. A few primitive
gravestones are scattered around; and there is a well in the
neighbourhood which was frequently resorted to on account
of its miraculous virtues.* In 1357 the chapel and its
pertinents, as we have seen, were granted by John of Menteith, Lord of Arran, to the Monks of Kilwinning. The
charter conveying the grant is witnessed by Saint Bean,
rector of St Mary. The patronage of Kilmorie appears to
have passed into the hands of the Hamilton family in
1503. †

The present Parish Church—a long, low, narrow building,
with Gothic windows—was built in 1785. There is a stone
font in the church-yard which may have belonged to the old
chapel.

On the farm of Balnacula, there lately existed the ruins of
a small cell belonging to a monk called John. The body
of the Saint is said to have been buried within the building.‡

The traditional Clachan of Saint Molios is supposed to
have occupied the site of the present chapel at Shiskin. It
is marked in Blæu's map as Kilmichael. The old church-
yard still remains with its primitive tombstones. Near its
centre there is the Stone of St Molios, said to have been
brought from Iona, sculptured with the figure of the Saint
arrayed in the robes of a mitred abbot, with pastoral staff
by his side and chalice in his hands.

* New Statistical Account.   † Ibid.
‡ Ibid.

Stone in Shiskin Church Yard.

The chalice is the symbol of an ecclesiastic, and the pastoral staff of a bishop or abbot; and these emblems of the sacerdotal dignity were occasionally buried with the deceased. "An ancient writer on ritual observances, cited by Martene, says that the bodies of persons who had received sacred orders, ought to be interred in the vestments worn by them at ordination; and that on the breast of a priest ought to be placed a chalice, which, in default of such sacred vessel of pewter, should be of earthenware." *

There is nothing improbable in the supposition that the body of Saint Molios may have been brought from Ireland, to the Island where he is said to have passed the early years of his manhood, and been buried there, in the little secluded cemetery of the Clachan. The Arran people fondly cling to the time-honoured traditions of their patron saint; and we would not rudely strip from the old burial-place the sacred halo, which has consecrated the dust of so many generations.

Within the present century, it was customary for females, after their confinement, to repair to the grave of the Saint, and deposit upon the stone a silver piece, as a thanks-offering for their recovery.†

Adjoining St Molios' tomb there are two slabs, apparently of some antiquity, incised with floral crosses, of neat and graceful design.

The ruins of a chapel, founded and endowed by Anne,

* Arch. Journal, Vol. III., p. 136.
† New Statistical Account.

Duchess of Hamilton, in aid of the parish church of Kilbride, recently stood on the margin of Lochranza. This was the legendary convent of Saint Bride, immortalised by Scott in his "Lord of the Isles." The arrival of Bruce at the convent, and the meeting with his sister, are thus beautifully and touchingly described by the poet:—

> "'Tis morning, and the Convent bell
> Long time had ceased its matin knell,
>   Within thy walls, Saint Bride!
> An aged sister sought the cell
> Assigned to Lady Isabel,
>   And hurriedly she cried,
> 'Haste, gentle lady, haste—there waits
> A noble stranger at the gates.'
>
> .   .   .   .
>
> They met like friends, who part in pain,
> And meet in doubtful hope again.
> And when subdued that fitful swell,
> The Bruce survey'd the humble cell;—
>   'And this is thine, poor Isabel!—
> That pallet-couch, and naked wall,
> For room of state, and bed of pall;
> For costly robes and jewels rare,
> A string of beads and zone of hair;
> And for the trumpet's sprightly call
> To sport or banquet, grove or hall,
> The bell's grim voice divides thy care,
> 'Twixt hours of penitence and prayer!'"*

But not a stone now remains of the cloisters where dwelt the lovely Isabel and the hapless Maid of Lorn.

---

* The Lord of the Isles, Canto IV.

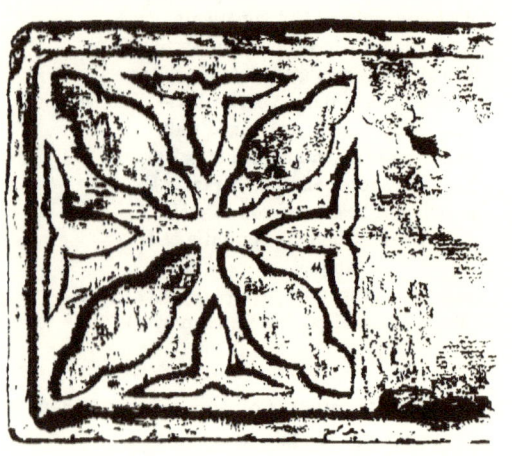

Stones in Shishkin Church Yard.

The modern church of Lochranza was built in 1795. It is an oblong building, seated to accommodate about 300 people.* There are some old gravestones in the churchyard, but their inscriptions are now entirely effaced.

* New Statistical Account.

CHAPTER IV.

WITH the exception of the farms of Kilmichael and White-farland, the Island of Arran is now the property of His Grace the Duke of Hamilton.

Its population in 1851 was 5947—Kilbride Parish 3414, and Kilmorie 2533. The Census just completed exhibits a decrease in these numbers,—the entire population being estimated at 5556.

Within the present century, the spirit of improvement has made rapid progress in Arran. Sixty years ago there was not a single road or bridge in the Island.* The people lived in the meanest hovels, and were clad in garments of the coarsest home manufacture. They possessed few educational advantages; the English language was but little known, and many of the older people were never taught to read.

The agricultural development of the soil was retarded by the rudeness of their husbandry implements, and the perni-cious system of farming which prevailed. Each farm was leased by five to ten families—constituting a kind of *societas arandi*—who were jointly and severally responsible for the

---

* Headrick's Arran.

payment of the rent. The fields were cultivated in common, and the rigs were exchanged every two years. Draining, manuring, and fencing were in consequence entirely neglected; and the scanty and stunted crops barely yielded their owners the necessary means of subsistence.

Illicit distillation and smuggling were occupations more congenial to the minds of the natives—the descendants of the Skotar-Gaels—than the unproductive drudgery of husbandry labour; and they who, amid darkness and tempest, could successfully steer their skiff, and land their cargoes unchallenged in the little hidden creek on the Ayrshire coast, were respected for their intrepidity and daring.

But all this is now changed. Excellent roads intersect and surround the Island; stone bridges span its streams, and instead of neglected rigs and heath-thatched hovels, many substantial farm-steadings and well-cultivated fields may be seen along the arable shorelands. Smuggling and illicit distillation have been rigorously suppressed.

The belief in fairies and witches, in the mysteries of Deuteroscopia or Second Sight, and in the power of the Evil Eye, still lingers in the minds of the older inhabitants; but the progress of education, and the facilities of communication with the mainland, have introduced amongst the Islanders the more practical and enlightened views of their Lowland neighbours, and given a finer polish to the native politeness, generosity, and manly independence of their character.

The Duke of Hamilton, who is warmly attached to Arran and the Arran people, has, during the last six years, expended

z

upwards of £2200 in the erection of schools for the children of his tenantry, besides contributing a considerable sum annually towards their endowment.   His Grace has also built handsome hotels at Brodick, Lag, and Corrie, for the convenience and comfort of visitors; and introduced many important improvements,—in the construction of bridges, enlarging of the farm-steadings, and in the formation of roads throughout the Island.

There are at present five churches and seven schools in the parish of Kilbride, and six churches and eight schools in that of Kilmorie.

Were it consistent with the views of its noble proprietor, the Island of Arran, with its salubrious climate, its magnificent scenery, its fine natural harbours, and its mineral wealth, might become one of the principal watering-places, and shipping and commercial marts, in the West of Scotland.*

* New Statistical Account.

INDEX.

GLASGOW: PRINTED BY THOMAS MURRAY AND SON.